Breed Lover's Guide™

BERNESE MOUNTAIN DOG

A Practical Guide for the Bernese Mountain Dog Lover

Linda Rehkopf

Bernese Mountain Dog

Project Team
Editor: Stephanie Fornino
Copy Editor: Joan Lowell Smith
Indexer: Elizabeth Walker
Design: Patricia Escabi

TFH Publications®
President/CEO: Glen S. Axelrod
Executive Vice President: Mark E. Johnson
Publisher: Christopher T. Reggio
Production Manager: Kathy Bontz

TFH Publications, Inc.®
One TFH Plaza
Third and Union Avenues
Neptune City, NJ 07753

Printed and bound in China
12 13 14 15 16 17   1 3 5 7 9 8 6 4 2

Library of Congress Cataloging-in-Publication Data
Rehkopf, Linda.
  Bernese mountain dog / Linda Rehkopf.
       p. cm
  Includes index.
  ISBN 978-0-7938-4184-4 (alk. paper)
  1. Bernese mountain dog. I. Title.
  SF429.B47R44 2012
  636.73--dc23
                              2011031276

The Leader In Responsible Animal Care For Over 50 Years!®
www.tfh.com

Table of Contents

History of Your
Bernese Mountain Dog

When the Romans invaded the area of modern-day Switzerland, they brought huge mastiff-like dogs who were strongly built and could bring down game or serve as guards for the army. The combination of size, strength, and watchfulness, along with duty to his family, are some of the hallmarks of today's Bernese Mountain Dog.

Early Development of the Breed

In the early years of the Swiss confederation, around 1350 CE, farmers in the area needed a dog who would help drive a few head of cattle from pasture to butcher, a dog who would warn his owner of approaching visitors or invaders, and a dog who would serve as a companion to the farmer and his family.

The dog needed to be just aloof enough that he was an "early warning system" but trustworthy enough around livestock and children. He needed an easily maintained coat but one that would protect him during the harsh winters. He also required stamina to help drive the few heads of cattle that the typical farmer owned. Like the Swiss people, he had to be sturdy,

The Bernese Mountain Dog hails from Switzerland.

By the early 1800s, the Swiss dogs were used to accompany their farmers to market, to announce strangers, and to keep small herds of cattle together.

aware of his surroundings, an affable host, and adaptable to the changing conditions in the midlands of Switzerland. In short, the Bernese Mountain Dog became a product of geography, climate, and the needs of his owners.

By the early 1800s, when most of the farms in the region were agriculture based, small, and far apart, the Swiss dogs, called Sennenhunds, were used to accompany the farmers to market, to announce strangers—people and other animals—by barking, and to keep the small herd of cattle together. The pastures in the region were neither large nor long distances away from the next grazing area, so dogs weren't required to drive large herds of cattle for long distances.

The Industrial Age

The Industrial Age brought major changes to Switzerland and surrounding areas, however. As dairy production developed and farming changed from grain-based agriculture to milk and cheese production farms, the dogs began to pull carts of milk and cheese to market. A large, well-muscled dog was required in this role. According to a *New York Times* article in 1893, dogs in harnesses, drawing carts and carriages, moved the vehicles with ease through the streets of Belgium.

Along with industrial developments, farms began to mechanize. The need to keep large, powerful animals to pull carts or carriages began to wane. Coupled with widespread poverty in the region, the family farm was in trouble. It became increasingly difficult for many farmers to justify keeping dogs, and by the late 19th century, the Sennenhund was almost extinct.

Saving the Breed

The Swiss fancier Franz Schertenleib began his search for good specimens for breeding stock, and the striking tricolored dog emerged among four main Swiss breeds: the Appenzeller, Entlebucher, Greater Swiss Mountain Dog, and a breed that came to be called the Duerbaechler.

Reportedly, Schertenleib purchased a dog from a region south of Bern called Duerbaech. The breeder continued to buy dogs from the same area, and his dogs became known as Duerbaechlers.

At around the same time, Professor Albert Heim of Zurich, a passionate dog fancier, turned his attention to the same four Swiss breeds. The striking appearance of the dog from Bern, along with the breed's temperament, attracted the respected dog show judge. Heim became a mentor to newcomers and a catalyst for breed recognition.

Formation of Breed Clubs

Purebred dog fanciers organized the Swiss Kennel Club, which was incorporated in 1883, a year before the American Kennel Club (AKC) was founded. By 1899, another Swiss dog club,

THE SWISS BREEDS IN THE UNITED STATES

Of the four "Swiss mountain breeds" recognized by the American Kennel Club (AKC), the Bernese Mountain Dog is the only one with long, silky hair. The other three breeds—the Appenzeller Sennenhund, the Entlebucher Sennenhund, and the Greater Swiss Mountain Dog—share some characteristics with the Berner, but they are each distinct either by coat, size, and/or markings. Known in his homeland as the Berner Sennenhund, the Bernese Mountain Dog breed came close to extinction in the late 1800s. Careful selection of breeding stock by fanciers allowed the breed to gain a small following in Europe. Imports of the breed from Switzerland to the United States began in earnest in the 1920s.

the Berna, was organized in Bern so that the widely scattered dog fanciers in the region could stay connected.

In 1899, when local innkeeper Fritz Probst of Bern exhibited his Duerbaechler in a dog show, the public saw and read the first newspaper accounts about the breed. Still, the tricolored dogs were exhibited on a limited basis only because so few of them existed. Weather and geography contributed to health problems of the large working dogs. Dogs at the famous St. Bernard Hospice in the Swiss Alps reportedly only lived, at most, eight years.

For the next couple of years, draft tests and breed specialties highlighted the dogs' versatility in still-limited exhibitions. Describing one such test in 1901, a columnist wrote that the "trial class for the Duerbaechler was well represented," with three specimens all from Bern.

The International Dog Show held in Bern in 1904 included classes for the Duerbaech dogs. The four winning Duerbaechlers were placed in the Swiss stud book, the first time the breed was recognized by the Swiss Kennel Club. Trial classes were then held for Duerbaechlers at the International Swiss Show, also in Bern. The judge, Fritz Probst, awarded four prizes to the classes, which included six Duerbaech dogs and one bitch.

The same year as the International Show, 1904, original fancier Schertenleib

The striking appearance of the dog from Bern, along with the breed's temperament, attracted the respected dog show judge Professor Albert Heim of Zurich.

exhibited the first Duerbaech dogs whom he called "Bernese," under his kennel name of Rothohe. The "Berner" name gained popularity among breeders and owners.

The First Breed Description
By 1907, a specialty club of Bernese Mountain Dog fans and breeders formed in the Burgdorf region. Members of the Schweizerischer Duerbaech Klub began

WILLING TO SERVE

Q: What draws you to the Bernese Mountain Dog rather than other breeds?

A: "Their kindness and gentleness. As a breed they have a very high 'will to serve.' Some breeds are all about the ME. A Berner was bred to be the farmer's companion dog; their job was to make their family or person happy, so their will to serve is high. They take that job very seriously."

—Amy Kessler, breeder, owner, and rescue coordinator

to write the first breed standard. The first detailed breed description, written by Heim, was published in the Swiss Kennel Club's magazine that year. The following year, the specialty Duerbaech Klub published its breed standard and changed its name to the Berner Sennenhund Club. Accordingly, the breed name was changed to Berner Sennenhund.

Breeders continued to develop the dog through the early 20th century as a companion dog, but the breed's working temperament and history as a watchdog remained its hallmark. While preserving those traits, judges began to award placements in dog shows to those breed representatives that had uniform markings.

Historical photographs show a large-boned dog with a silky, wavy coat and the characteristic white chest blaze and white toes and tan- or rust-colored stockings. The stocking markings were not always uniform from dog to dog. The current white face blaze isn't readily apparent on the early dogs—only a white muzzle ring around the nose.

The Ban on Cart Dogs

Despite the growing popularity of the Bernese Mountain Dog and other native Swiss working dogs, the breed took a hit in 1910 when Belgium enacted a ban on cart dogs because of the growing popularity of motor cars and trucks. However, people who depended on cart dogs for their livelihood were granted an exemption, so the breeds endured. Indeed, fanciers of the Swiss breeds began to organize, breed, and exhibit their stock in dog shows. The Belgian government reversed its ban on cart dogs in 1912, when comparison tests showed that a draft dog could pull machine guns more effectively than a horse. The Belgian army began using draft dogs rather than horses or other livestock.

In 1910, Belgium enacted a ban on cart dogs because of the growing popularity of motor cars and trucks.

The so-called "Belgian cart dog ordinance" was permanently suspended in 1914, when Germany invaded Belgium during World War I. The war, however, took a terrible toll not just on dogs and dog shows but also on the fanciers in Europe. Not until the 1920s did the Bernese Mountain Dog rebound with pre-war numbers of registrations with the Swiss Kennel Club. In 1922, there were 58 such registrations.

International Recognition

International recognition followed quickly, though, under the banner of the Fédération Cynologique Internationale (FCI), which governs dog shows and encourages official breed standards to be written and adopted among member national clubs. The first Berners were imported to Holland in 1924, a German Bernese club was formed and affiliated with the FCI in 1925, and the Bernese Mountain Dog was introduced to the United States in 1926.

A Kansas farmer, Isaac Schiess, imported the bitch Donna von der Rothohe, a product of Swiss fancier Franz Schertenleib's Rothohe kennels. He also imported the dog Poincare von Sumiswald. Neither of these two dogs was registered with the AKC. Likewise, their first litter of puppies wasn't recognized by the AKC but was accepted and registered by the Swiss Kennel Club under the Clover Leaf kennel prefix.

Popularity and puppy whelping continued through Europe, with fanciers in Great Britain importing and breeding Berners in the 1930s. American breeders also imported dogs from Switzerland.

American Kennel Club (AKC) Breed Recognition

A Louisiana breeder, Glen Shadow, imported stock in 1936; the following year, the AKC officially recognized the Bernese Mountain Dog as a new breed in the Working Group.

Shadow's Fridy v. Haslenbach and Quell v. Tiergarten, his Swiss imports, became the first Bernese Mountain Dogs registered by the AKC in the United States.

TIMELINE

- **1850:** The Swiss farm dog is described in a work of literature, *Michael's Search for a Wife*, by the author Jeremias Gotthelf.
- **1853:** In another publication, author F.V. Tschundy writes about a medium-sized dog used by Swiss herdsmen to keep the herds together and to protect the family's dwellings.
- **1893:** The Swiss Kennel Club is founded, and F.V. Tschundy is responsible for the stud book.
- **1899:** The Berna, a Swiss dog club, is founded in Bern for fanciers. Albert Heim is an early breed enthusiast and mentor.
- **1899:** Breed recognition is gained in Switzerland.
- **1904:** International Dog Show is held in Bern, and the local club sponsors a class for Swiss "shepherd dogs," along with Appenzeller Sennenhunds and Duerbaech dogs.
- **1904:** The first dogs referred to as "Bernese" were exhibited under the kennel prefix Rothohe.
- **1905:** Four Duerbaech are placed in the Swiss stud book, signaling breed recognition by the Swiss Kennel Club.
- **1908:** Duerbaech Klub publishes a breed standard.
- **1908:** Duerbaechler Klub changes its name to Berner Sennenhund Club, and the breed name is changed to Berner Sennenhund.
- **1910:** Belgium enacts total ban on cart dogs, except for those whose livelihoods depend on the dogs; this helps the dogs to develop and endure as a breed until the start of World War I.
- **1914–1918:** World War I years; when Germany invades Belgium in 1914, experienced cart dogs are confiscated for military use.
- **1926:** The breed is introduced to the United States. The first litter, from Clover Leaf Kennel, is refused American Kennel Club (AKC) registration but is recognized by the Swiss Kennel Club.
- **1937:** Fancier Glen Shadow in Louisiana receives first AKC letter of breed recognition for the Bernese Mountain Dog; the breed is placed in the Working Group. The AKC breed standard is adopted from the Swiss standard.
- **1949:** Mr. Shadow is listed as the only AKC-registered breeder of Bernese Mountain Dogs.
- **1956:** The Swiss Kennel Club introduces temperament testing for all breeding stock.

- **1962:** The first AKC title earned by a Bernese Mountain Dog is a Companion Dog (CD) obedience title.
- **1968:** The Bernese Mountain Dog Club of America (BMDCA) is founded with 62 members.
- **1968:** The first breed champion in the United States is Ch. Sanctuary Woods Black Knight, owned by Roberta Subin and bred by Beatrice Knight.
- **1969:** The Bernese Mountain Dog is reintroduced in Great Britain, where the breed had all but disappeared after World War II.
- **1971:** A parent club is organized in Great Britain.
- **1971:** The first Companion Dog Excellent (CDX) is earned by a Bernese Mountain Dog.
- **1972:** The AKC accepts the BMDCA constitution and bylaws and approves the first Berner "B" match in the United States.
- **1973:** The BMDCA is named an AKC-sanctioned club.
- **1974:** The BMDCA is named an AKC-licensed club and holds the first "A" matches.
- **1976:** The first Berner tracking title is earned by Ch. Tanja V Nesselacker CD TD.
- **1976:** The BMDCA holds its first national specialty.
- **1977:** The first AKC Best in Show Bernese Mountain Dog is Ch. Alphorn's Copyright of Echo.
- **1977:** The Canadian Kennel Club (CKC) recognizes the breed.
- **1979:** The AKC revises the breed standard.
- **1979:** Ch. Dina De L'Armary UD earns the AKC Utility Dog obedience title.
- **1979:** The BMDCA develops draft test regulations.
- **1981:** The BMDCA earns member club status in the AKC.
- **1985:** Ch. Shersan Change O'Pace v. Halidom wins the Westminster Kennel Club Working Group.
- **1985:** Viva's Graemlicher Bischoff TDX earns the Tracking Dog Excellent title.
- **1990:** The second revision to the US standard is written and adopted by the AKC.
- **1990:** Berners compete in agility for the first time at a national specialty demonstration.
- **1992:** Two Bernese Mountain dogs earn Draft Dog titles.
- **1995:** Berner-Garde, a registry to track health issues and stud dogs in the breed, incorporates.
- **1996:** Twenty-six Versatility Awards are granted by the BMDCA.
- **2010:** The Bernese Mountain Dog climbs the AKC's "popularity" ladder with a jump to 39th most popular breed, up from 47th in 2005.

The AKC adopted the FCI breed standard, which highlights the dog's working heritage. Indeed, the first AKC title earned by a Bernese Mountain Dog was the Companion Dog (CD) obedience title given to Aya of Verlap. This obedience title showcases a dog's ability to work alongside and respond to commands from his handler, a trait that the breed perfected over generations of working next to its farmer.

Breeders in the United States had loose-knit groups around the country, but in 1962 the AKC listed only nine owners in the United States. Devotees of the breed decided to organize a national breed club, formally organizing as the Bernese Mountain Dog Club of America (BMDCA) in 1968. Club members worked hard during the late 1960s and early 1970s to develop a constitution, bylaws, and breeder ethics, as well as hold matches and fun days. In 1975, the parent club was granted AKC permission to hold independent specialties, which are shows just for Bernese Mountain Dogs. The first Bernese Mountain Dog Club of American National Specialty was held in Harrisburg, Pennsylvania.

It took the club until 1981, after the successful completion of six specialties, to gain member club status with the AKC. Member status meant that the parent club

Not until the 1920s did the Bernese Mountain Dog rebound with pre-war numbers of registrations with the Swiss Kennel Club.

WHAT IS A BREED CLUB?

A breed club is a group of breed fanciers that forms to keep and write the official breed standard; hold matches, shows, and puppy socialization opportunities; and agree to breed litters only to advance, or improve, the breed. Members might be active breeders or might compete only in one of the companion or performance sports like obedience or drafting. They also agree to mentor newcomers to the sport of purebred dogs. Some breed clubs have active rescue groups and work hard to rehome those dogs who have been found in shelters and puppy mills or turned in by owners who cannot keep their dogs.

Breed clubs disseminate accurate information about their breed. The Bernese Mountain Dog Club of America (BMDCA), the "parent breed club," has a comprehensive website—www.bmdca.org—that includes information about the breed, resources for new puppy owners, a list of ethical breeders, and information about the breed's health issues.

would have a delegate voice at the AKC, and Mary Jo Thomson was named the club's first delegate.

While working toward member club status, fanciers continued to breed, train, exhibit, and compete with their Bernese Mountain Dogs. The affable dogs earned championships, obedience titles, agility titles, and tracking titles. The BMDCA held the first draft test in 1991, with seven dogs earning the Novice Draft Dog title. In 2010, the AKC allowed Berners to earn that registry's herding titles, and in 2011, the AKC began allowing titles earned in BMDCA draft tests as official AKC awards.

Much as retrievers, spaniels, setters, and pointers have AKC hunt titles to work toward, the Bernese Mountain Dog fanciers expect that their dogs' heritage as drafters and drovers will lead to more Berners competing and earning draft titles.

The Bernese Mountain Dog was introduced to the United States in 1926.

Chapter
2

Characteristics of Your Bernese Mountain Dog

The characteristics of the Bernese Mountain Dog, bred to help farmers in the prealpine regions of Switzerland, highlight the dog's role as friend, cart puller, herding dog, and a watchdog for his family.

From his long, thick coat to his intelligence and companionability, the breed obviously has a background as a hardworking dog in cold climates. His structure and size allow the Bernese Mountain Dog to pull heavy loads or impress strangers or unwelcome visitors. His temperament is confident and calm enough to herd stock as small as a duck and as large as a dairy cow. His devotion to his family, especially children and other household pets, makes the breed a wonderful addition to modern homes.

Physical Characteristics of Your Berner

The breed standard, which is a description of the ideal Bernese Mountain Dog, puts a premium on a sturdy dog with good, heavy bones.

Size

The Bernese Mountain Dog is a large, heavy-boned dog who can weigh from about 90 pounds (41 kg) to as much as 120 pounds (55 kg), in good condition. While an individual dog's weight can vary, of course, depending upon gender and health, this is a muscular dog with very little fat. A bitch (or female dog) should be from 23 inches (58.5 cm) up to 26 inches (66 cm) at the withers, or shoulders. The male dog's height at the withers should be 25 inches (63.5 cm) up to 27.5 inches (70 cm).

His thick coat can fool people into thinking the Bernese Mountain Dog is square, or about the same height at the withers as the dog is long. However, he should measure a bit longer from the withers to the tail set than his height.

The Bernese Mountain Dog has a background as a hardworking dog in cold climates.

Everything about the Bernese's bodily structure should indicate strength.

Body Structure

This breed has a strong neck, and his topline is level from the length of his withers to his croup, where his tail starts. He has a deep chest that reaches down at least to his elbows, if not farther. The Bernese Mountain Dog doesn't have a barrel-shaped chest, but it is broad, as is his back. Everything about this dog should indicate strength.

Ears

His ears, which can have some feathering, are set high on his head and are relaxed and close to the head if he is not alerted to something. The triangle-shaped ears are rounded at the tips. If the dog is interested or alarmed, he will bring his ears forward and raise them a bit from the base so that the top of the ears are level with the top of his head.

Expression and Eyes

The Bernese Mountain Dog's expression is as important as his color. He should appear intelligent, with a gentle and animated face. His dark brown eyes are a bit oval, and his eyelids should not droop but rather fit closely to his eyes.

A dog who has blue eyes would be disqualified in the conformation ring but would still be an eager family pet or canine sport participant.

Ask the Expert

BERNER TRAITS

Q: What breed-specific trait stands out about the Bernese Mountain Dog?

A: "Their size! I think most people see them and think they are bigger (weight wise) than they are. I have people look at them and think they are 150 pounds (68 kg), but in actuality they are 100 to 110 pounds (45.5 to 50 kg). Also, their gentleness and kindness. Some people call them needy, but it is their need to make sure that you are happy."

—Amy Kessler, breeder, owner, and rescue coordinator

Head

The Berner's head is flat on top, level and broad. The head should have a well-defined stop, or slope from the skull to the muzzle, but the stop is not extreme. His muzzle is straight, strong, and ends with a jet black nose.

Legs and Feet

A Bernese Mountain Dog's rear legs must be strong enough to do the work he was bred to perform, with broad, muscular thighs. He should have only a moderate bend in his stifles, or knee joints. The hocks are straight. Like his front feet, the rear feet are compact and should face straight forward. The feet should not turn out or turn in, as this could impede the dog's propulsion. The feet are compact, round, and have toes that arch up.

The Berner's shoulders lie flat with strong muscles that work tightly with his strong, straight front legs. When standing, the Berner's elbows are under the shoulder. His pasterns, or the section of leg from the ankle to the front feet, might slope just a bit, but again are very strong.

His rear dewclaws—an extra claw at the rear ankle joints—are usually removed when the pup is just days old because they can catch and rip when he romps or plays with another dog. Some specimens have double dewclaws. Front dewclaws don't usually cause the same injury concerns and aren't removed.

This breed works at a slow trot, but he can travel much faster. His power, which is driven from his strong rear legs and maintained through his level back, provides good extension of his front legs. If the dog is watched from the side, the front and rear legs on the same side will follow through in the same plane. Once the dog picks up speed, his legs may converge at the centerline of his body.

Obviously, a dog this powerful does not exert his energy with action or movement that is wasted.

Mouth
A Bernese Mountain Dog does not have pendulous lips, or flews, and the lips are clean. This is not an overly drooly dog. He should not be missing any teeth, and they should meet in a scissors bite. Teeth that are undershot or overshot are serious faults.

Nose
Puppies are not born with a black nose or pads, but by two months of age, the nose has turned from its newborn-pink coloring to all black. The pads might take a bit longer to turn color.

Tail
The Berner's rear is broad, rounding off at his tail set. The tail reaches down to his hock joint, at least, and could be longer but should never kink. When the dog is

A Bernese Mountain Dog's rear legs must be strong enough to do the work he was bred to perform, with broad, muscular thighs.

The stunning tricolored Berner is black, white, and rust.

excited or alert, he might carry his tail up, but it shouldn't curl or sway over his back. When he is relaxed, his tail is low. A happy Bernese Mountain Dog will swing his tail slowly back and forth, and it's strong enough to clear a coffee table.

Coat Type

This large dog can appear bigger than he really is, due to his thick coat. Unlike the other so-called "Swiss breeds," the Berner has a long, silky, soft coat. The coat is either straight or wavy but should also have a natural shine. Some dogs sport curly coats, which was quite common in the late 1800s and early 1900s. Today,

while not a disqualifying fault, this coat type is not considered desirable for dogs in the conformation ring. Those Bernese Mountain Dogs with a curly coat can go on to have extraordinary careers in canine sports or as special family companions.

Coat Colors

The colors on this stunning tricolored dog make him instantly recognizable. His base color is jet black. His broad chest is marked with a thick white bib, which some refer to as the "Swiss cross." This bib color matches the white-tipped tail; his toes and feet also are white, but the color should not extend higher than the dog's pasterns. He also has a white band around his muzzle and a white blaze up the center of his face. Some individual dogs have freckles, or small black or rust flecks, within the white muzzle band and within the face blaze. These freckles give the dog an impish, comical expression, matching a Berner's clownish temperament.

The rust color on his legs gives the appearance of a symmetrical stocking-and-glove effect. The rust also appears over each eye, on his cheeks, to the corners of his grinning mouth, along the edges of the chest blaze, and under his tail.

For conformation dogs, the only coat disqualification is a base color that is not black.

These are the markings that early breed fanciers prized and that judges rewarded over dogs who didn't show symmetrical markings.

Temperament

Even though the Bernese Mountain Dog is a working breed and as such might be aloof, his temperament is good natured and even loving toward strangers. He should always be alert and steady with his owner and never shy away from visitors. Because the available gene pool of mating dogs is smaller than some more popular breeds, shyness has become a temperament issue in this breed. However, shy puppies or young adult dogs can be trained and socialized so that they are more comfortable in unfamiliar surroundings or among visitors.

Living With Your Berner

Every Bernese Mountain Dog owner will tell newcomers to the breed that this is an affectionate dog, gentle and kind. Once a Berner bonds with his person or family, he will do anything to make them laugh and be happy and feel secure. These funny, loving, devoted, and beautiful dogs fit into most family situations, in

Puppy Love

A WELL-MANNERED DOG

A healthy puppy can begin basic obedience and manners training at eight weeks of age. This is a breed that should learn to be friendly toward people long before the puppy grows up. A well-mannered dog is the ultimate goal of any puppy socialization or training class, and this is especially important with a breed as large as a Berner, who typically retains his "puppy brain" until he's about a year and a half old.

most locations, and in most any setting. Whether one wants a couch potato and foot-warmer or a dog who will take long, slow hikes in the country, the Berner seems made for any job.

However, prospective Bernese Mountain Dog owners need to be prepared to invest huge sums into care, training, feeding, and veterinary costs. The tradeoffs, however, make these dogs worth every penny.

Personality

Most Bernese Mountain Dogs are biddable, which means that they will willingly go along with their owner's plans. If those plans include fun, then the Berner is all in! They can be silly and serious, clown-like and composed. The Bernese Mountain Dog's personality is one of the most-loved aspects of the breed. They seem to consider themselves the center of the family and just want to be with their people. Companionship is an important hallmark of this breed, and a Berner can express his joy in any number of ways.

The "Berner hug" is the dog's typical greeting, whether his owner has just gone to the mailbox or has been away for days. This loveable dog will jump up and wrap his front paws around his owner's upper body. While this might be a cute trick for a grown dog and a grown owner, if the dog isn't trained when he is young and small,

that "hug" can potentially harm a smaller, innocent visitor or owner, or a child.

A Berner also loves to get close and do the "Berner lean" and put all his weight against his owner while keeping all four paws on the floor. He will sit on his owner's feet to be as physically close as possible. He would hang from his owner's apron strings if allowed, rest his big head on her bed pillows at night, and follow her into the bathroom at every opportunity.

Athleticism

Once a puppy's basic training has been completed, the Berner can be taught to do a number of tasks or compete in canine sports. Versatility could be the Bernese Mountain Dog's middle name, and several venues exist to show off the breed's capabilities.

Many Bernese Mountain dogs perform at high levels of obedience competition and easily learn to handle the obstacles in agility. But this large dog should never attempt fast, repetitive jumping that could injure his joints. Also, Berners are not the fastest dogs on an agility course, so this might not be the right breed for people who aim to compete at high levels in agility.

This breed excels at tracking. Teaching a Bernese Mountain Dog to follow a track is another activity that doesn't put quite the stress on the dog's joints as, say, obedience and agility jumping do.

Training, fun, and canine competitions also exist in sports that mimic the breed's heritage, specifically drafting and herding. Draft dogs are trained to pull a cart or wagon, either alone or alongside another dog. Herding instincts can be tested on a variety of stock, from fowl to cattle. Newcomers to draft and herding tests are welcome at events around the United States. Many of these tests are hosted by regional Bernese Mountain Dog clubs or by the national parent club.

The Bernese Mountain Dog Club of America (BMDCA) encourages its members to explore a variety of training and competition activities. The club awards Draft Dog (carting) titles, and Bernese Mountain Dogs are also accepted into herding trials organized by the American Herding Breed Association (AHBA) and the American Kennel Club (AKC).

Versatility and Working Dog titles are club awards given to dogs who have excelled at multiple sports, from conformation to carting. Members and dogs who train and title in at least three canine sports are lauded by the club at an awards ceremony each year.

Because the Bernese Mountain Dog is so gentle, he is typically very good with children.

Companionability

These so-called confident dogs are actually very dependent and needy with their owners. A minute apart, after all, is a minute not spent in their owner's presence. A Berner wants, more than anything, to be with his owner. Before thinking about bringing home a Bernese Mountain Dog, prospective owners should carefully consider if they want a large dog who can be clingy.

With Strangers

Although Bernese Mountain dogs are initially aloof with strangers, once the dog warms up to a visitor, she also might find a Berner snoozing on her feet by the end of a social visit. Or the dog might choose to join the conversation and make his own comments in his particular Berner vernacular, grumbling one moment and squeaking the next.

With Animals and Children

Because the Bernese Mountain Dog is so gentle, he is typically very good with other animals and with children. A well-bred dog is alert, confident, and good natured, never shy nor sharp toward other animals or children. The Berner grows quickly to become a large dog, however, which means that owners must provide adequate training for the dog and supervise interactions between the dog and children.

Even working herding Berners take great care with the smallest charge. "One of my dogs loves to herd ducks, but when the ducks don't go in the direction she is sending them, she bends down and bowls them with her nose, ever so gently, in the right direction," said one owner.

Young children should never be left with a puppy or adult Bernese Mountain Dog without strict parental supervision. Children need to be taught how to behave around dogs of any breed, and the Berner is no exception. Accidents happen when strict rules of engagement are not followed or enforced between children and growing dogs.

With Other Dogs

Bernese Mountain Dog owners are quick to point out that many households have more than one of the big dogs because they are so addictive. "You can't have just one," is said by many in the breed. Indeed, the Bernese Mountain Dog craves attention and affection and often does not tolerate living alone or as an "only dog." Socially and

BERNERS AND CHILDREN

Although Berners are wonderful family companions, young children should never be left unsupervised with the breed, even as a puppy. Both the kids and the dog can be inadvertently injured by inappropriate play. Even though this is a large breed, Berner puppies, in particular, are delicate. Rough play or too long of a playtime can injure the growing bones and muscles of a Bernese Mountain Dog pup.

temperamentally, a Berner thrives in a home with other animals, especially other Berners.

Environment

Prospective owners in metropolitan and dense urban areas aren't dismissed due to space constraints. As long as apartment, condo, and townhouse owners aren't bothered by the living arrangements with a large dog, plan their space wisely, and budget enough time for appropriate play and exercise, a Berner can do well in smaller homes.

Small suburban fenced yards might not provide the room that a mature Berner needs to get adequate exercise. If a family provides the amount of exercise necessary, has a fenced yard big enough for the Bernese Mountain Dog to retreat to daily for some fresh air and a fun romp, and allows him to live inside the home, the Berner is likely to do well.

As a large working breed, the Bernese Mountain Dog's heritage was developed on the rural farm, so naturally he does very well in rural environments.

Whatever the family's living arrangement, though, their Bernese Mountain Dog needs to live inside the house with his people. They don't do well outside in a kennel or dog run, nor should a Berner ever spend his life tied to a tree.

Once a puppy's basic training has been completed, the Berner can be taught to do a number of tasks or compete in canine sports.

Exercise

To stay fit both physically and mentally, this breed needs a good bit of moderate exercise daily, punctuated by more vigorous activity. A brisk walk every day, rain or shine, in snowstorms, blizzards and monsoons, gives the Berner an outlet for his high energy. His work ethic needs to be nurtured, so his owner should be home to take him to a dog park or on leashed walks. She should also consider participating in canine sports with her dog.

Their heavy black coats make them susceptible to extreme heat, which is a good reason why the Bernese Mountain Dog should live in a climate-controlled area. They can acclimate to warmer environments, but their exercise periods should be limited to the cooler mornings or evenings.

Life Span

As wonderful as this breed is, and as capable as he performs, the one heartache that every Berner owner will face is the short life span of this beloved dog. Large and giant breed dogs typically do not live as long as smaller breeds. The Bernese Mountain Dog is no exception.

Many owners say the hardest part of owning this breed is the knowledge that a well-loved dog will be taken way too soon. The average life span of the Bernese Mountain Dog is about 8 years, but many individual dogs live as long as 12 to 14 years.

Trainability

Berners readily take to positive training methods, and the earlier a puppy's training begins, the more control an owner will have when that cuddly puppy grows up into his adult frame.

Because this breed was developed from dogs who worked various jobs on farms alongside the farmer, Berners generally try to do what is asked of them. Individually, there are select stubborn dogs who need more persuasion than others, and others are downright lazy.

Training a Berner does not involve multiple repetitions of the same task, however. He will usually perform a training task once or twice and then decide that he's done. Trainers must stay a step ahead of these creative dogs by providing stimulating opportunities for training and socialization.

Most breeders suggest that Berner puppies should begin their formal education with

Socially and temperamentally, a Berner thrives in a home with other animals, especially other Berners.

Check It Out

BREED FACTS

- ✓ Bernese Mountain Dogs grow to be large dogs.
- ✓ The Berner has a thick, long, silky coat.
- ✓ Some dogs reach a height of 27 inches (68.5 cm) and weigh more than 100 pounds (45.5 kg).
- ✓ The jet-black coat is marked with rust-colored legs, white feet and muzzle ring, white forehead blaze, and the classic "Swiss cross" white chest bib.
- ✓ The dog has strong muscles from neck to stifles.
- ✓ The Berner's heritage as a working farm dog is reflected in his aloof temperament with strangers.
- ✓ Shyness has been noted as a problem among some individual puppies.
- ✓ A Berner lives to please his people and will often act like the class clown.
- ✓ Bernese Mountain Dogs thrive in a home with other dogs, cats, and children.
- ✓ Room to roam, exercise, and play makes rural homes ideal for this breed.
- ✓ Berners in warm climates need protection from the heat and humidity.
- ✓ A Bernese Mountain Dog requires vigorous daily exercise.
- ✓ A Berner puppy should begin manners training at an early age.
- ✓ This breed responds to positive training methods.
- ✓ Bernese Mountain dogs excel at carting and herding activities.
- ✓ Bernese Mountain Dogs are not long-lived. The average life span is about eight years.
- ✓ The costs for training, feeding, and veterinary care can be substantial with the Bernese Mountain Dog.

basic puppy socialization, also known as "puppy kindergarten" class. Basic obedience training is necessary to teach household manners. An unruly puppy who is not trained properly will grow up to be an large, unruly dog. The main reasons that dogs are surrendered to shelters are the excuses: "He won't behave" or "He's too rough with my children." A Berner deserves more than surrender to a rescue or shelter because his owner didn't take the time to train or socialize him.

Watchdog Ability

Even though historically the Bernese Mountain Dog served as a watchdog, this breed should never be aggressive. Rather, a Berner is a careful watcher, a dog who pays attention, really noticing what is going on around him. His bark is more likely an announcement than a warning.

Chapter
3

Supplies for Your Bernese Mountain Dog

Bernese Mountain Dogs are mighty big. Correspondingly, all the supplies that a Bernese Mountain Dog needs must be big. Keep in mind that a Berner puppy grows fast, so all his "stuff," from bowls to crates to brushes, needs to accommodate his size. Because the supplies have to be large, the costs will be considerably more than those for a much smaller dog. Be prepared to invest many dollars in a Berner's upkeep and maintenance.

Your puppy's breeder will make recommendations on what to purchase. A wise owner will follow that advice. Here are some thoughts on supplies that every well-loved Bernese Mountain Dog will need:

Baby Gates

Baby gates or dog gates are more than tools to restrict your Bernese Mountain Dog from areas of your home. Properly used, a gate can keep your sofa from being shredded down to the frame by a Berner who is bored. Because Bernese Mountain Dogs are not frantic fence jumpers, even a 2-foot-high (.5-m) gate placed across an access area will keep them confined.

If you are training your dog to stay behind a barrier, like a baby gate, go

If you don't want your Berner on the furniture while you're not home, a baby gate or crate may be the answer.

DNA PROFILE

The Bernese Mountain Dog Club of America (BMDCA) requires that any Berner competing in one of the club's conformation, performance, and companion sports, along with drafting and herding tests, must have a DNA profile. The testing kit, which can be ordered from the American Kennel Club (AKC) at www.akc.org, is another form of permanent identification. The club uses DNA tests to prove a dog's parentage. Other DNA tests can bank tissue for current and future health studies that track problems with Bernese Mountain Dogs. For more information on the club's required DNA tests, go to www.bmdca.org.

slowly. Dogs must be acclimated to a gate. If done too quickly or improperly, you're likely to find that the dog has crashed the gate with his strength and reached the family heirlooms.

To train a dog to respect the gate, put it across a doorway between you and the dog. Give him some time to sniff this new "toy," and be liberal with praise and treats. Practice standing on the opposite side of the gate and giving him commands that he may already know, such as the *sit* or *down*. (See Chapter 6 for instructions on how to teach these cues.) With every successful repetition—which for a Berner might be only one or two commands—toss a tasty treat or a favorite toy over his head. He'll come to look forward to this new "game."

Don't expect a determined Bernese Mountain Dog to stay behind a gate, however. If your dog is unreliable and won't stay off the furniture or out of your makeup while you are away from home, then a baby gate isn't the answer. Keep him in his crate during absences rather than relying on a gate to keep him safe.

Bed

He's likely to want to sleep in bed with his humans, but that may not be practical for the owner of a Bernese Mountain Dog. If you want to purchase a dog bed, look for those that will support the joints of a large-breed dog. Thick orthopedic foam core, surrounded by a durable, washable cover, is the best type of bed for the Berner. Many dog beds on the market are more durable than others, so take the time to examine the product. Flimsy beds with loose filling are likely to be chewed up, and if not swallowed by the dog, strewn throughout the house.

Collar

Breeders might send their puppies to their new homes already sporting a collar. If not, don't spend a ton of money for a puppy's collar that he might grow out of within a few weeks. Bernese Mountain Dog puppies don't need glitter, silver studs, gold spikes, or other embellishments on the collar. Rather, a flat buckle collar that will adjust to a puppy's rapidly growing neck circumference is the better choice.

Once a Berner has reached physical maturity, a sturdier collar is necessary. The options vary for the grown-up Bernese Mountain Dog. Rolled bridle leather collars don't snag or tear at a dog's fur like some other materials. This is a great option for owners who think that their dog might compete in the conformation ring. Flat collars will flatten a dog's neck fur, so keep the Berner's future show career in mind when purchasing a collar.

For those Bernese Mountain Dogs who grow up to be wonderful household pets or compete in other canine sports, a flat collar with a secure buckle is just fine. As

For those Bernese Mountain Dogs who grow up to be household pets or compete in other canine sports, a flat collar with a secure buckle is just fine.

long as the collar is adjustable and does not constrict the still-growing neck, is not cheaply made, and has strong rings to attach a leash and the dog's tags, you'll have options.

Embroidered collars showing off the dog's Swiss heritage are popular and can be found at many high-end pet supply catalogs or stores.

Puppy Love

COLLAR SIZE

Bernese Mountain Dog puppies grow quickly. A collar should fit snugly enough that the puppy cannot wriggle out of it but not too tightly that it constricts the puppy. To check for the proper fit, insert two fingers between the collar and the pup's neck; if your fingers slide easily, the collar may be too big. If your fingers feel tight, then either adjust the collar or buy the next size up.

Crate

A crate is the single most important piece of equipment that a Bernese Mountain Dog owner will purchase for her dog. The crate is also likely to be the most expensive.

Crates serve multiple purposes. In a busy household with children, a dog who has his own crate can retreat when the home gets too hectic. If he needs a break from the children or a safe place, the Berner who is crate trained will see his crate as a refuge. And housetraining a Berner puppy will progress more rapidly if a crate is utilized. A crate is also perfect for long car trips. A Bernese Mountain Dog settled safely in a crate won't become a 100-pound (45.5-kg) missile during a traffic accident.

Shopping for a crate can be done in person or online, but there are some important considerations to keep in mind when selecting the right one for your dog.

Nylon/Canvas Crates

Because puppies chew, a nylon or canvas crate is not the best "first crate" for a Bernese Mountain Dog. These crates can easily roll if a determined Berner decides he wants to move around. If you decide to invest in one of these types of crates, wait until your Berner is more crate reliable and will settle quickly and quietly. He should also be at the point where he refrains from using zippers, flaps, or fabric as a chew toy.

Plastic Crates

Airline-approved plastic crates can give a shy, fearful, or young puppy a sense of protection. These crates should have ample ventilation from front to back and from side to side. Because of the cost, plan to get the largest size possible, one that will accommodate the grown Berner. You can always block off a portion of the crate while your dog is still a puppy to prevent him from soiling one area of the enclosure and then resting comfortably in another.

If you want to purchase a dog bed, look for those that will support the joints of a large-breed dog.

Wire Crates

Heavy wire crates are popular because grates can be attached to expand the inside area as the puppy grows. Some models will collapse "suitcase style," which is handy for a Berner who travels with his family. Most hotels that allow dogs also require that the dog remain in a crate in the room. Wire crates allow for maximum air ventilation, but they can also be covered with a lightweight blanket or sheet to give the dog privacy.

Ex-Pen

An ex-pen, short for exercise pen, is a nylon or wire pen that folds up. These pens come in different heights and lengths and can be attached to make a very large enclosure. The ex-pen can be set up in the front yard, the living room, or on a deck and allow the Berner to still be "with his people" but not underfoot.

A puppy should be conditioned to an ex-pen, just as you've done with the baby gate, and taught not to jump up on the sides. The wire pens are not terribly

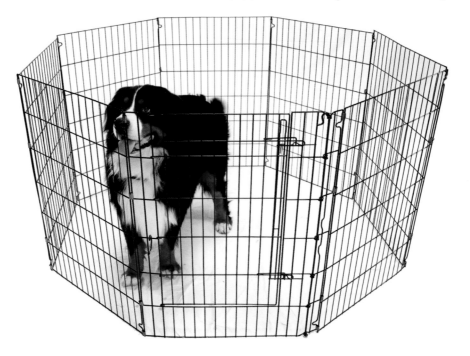

An ex-pen allows the Berner to hang out with his family but remain out of the way.

THE MUST-HAVE GROOMING TOOL

Q: What one grooming tool is a must have, something you could not live without?

A: "A coat rake!"

—Amy Kessler, breeder, owner, and rescue coordinator

sturdy, and a determined Berner could easily bowl the pen over on his way to greet his favorite folks.

Food and Water Bowls

Food and water bowls for a Bernese Mountain Dog need to be large. Stainless steel bowls are the easiest to clean and can be put in a dishwasher. Typically the least expensive, stainless steel bowls are also the most indestructible. If your Bernese Mountain Dog likes to play, not only with his food but with his bowls, stainless is more forgiving. Plan to buy several bowls so that the dirty ones can be rotated out with clean bowls on a regular basis.

Some canine nutritionists and veterinarians believe that plastic or ceramic bowls may leach toxins into a dog's food and water. Because Bernese Mountain Dogs are prone to cancer, there's no good reason to add to the list of possible causes by using inexpensive plastic or improperly fired and glazed ceramic bowls. Additionally, ceramic

bowls are breakable, and plastic bowls can incur microscopic cracks, which can harbor bacteria.

Grooming Tools

A double-coated breed, the Berner sheds heavily on a regular basis. Regular grooming with the proper tools will help maintain the coat, prevent matting, alert the owner to any health problems that might be hidden by the long coat, and provide both dog and owner with some one-on-one time to bond.

Coat Tools

Essential coat grooming tools include a wide-toothed steel comb, a de-shedding rake or blade to remove undercoat as it sheds, and a good stiff bristle brush.

The comb is used to tease out any tangles or mats from the delicate leg feathers and around the ears. The rake has teeth that are widely spread, helpful to brush out the thick undercoat year round but especially during a Berner's heaviest shed period.

A quality brush with stiff bristles, either metal pin style or natural bristle, is used on the coat after raking and combing.

Dental and Ear Care Products

Grooming a Bernese Mountain Dog should include dental and ear care products.

Canine-specific toothpaste, using either a toothbrush or finger brush, should be applied at least a few times a week and ideally on a daily basis. Tartar control is an important part of a dog's well-being, as dental disease can lead to whole-body illnesses. A tooth scaler is helpful to keep a Berner's molars free of plaque buildup. Ask your groomer, veterinarian, or vet tech to show you the proper use of a scaler.

For ear cleaning, several products are available from pet supply stores. An alternative is a homemade solution of equal parts water and peroxide, which flushes the ear canal, followed by a solution of water and rubbing alcohol, which helps dry the ear canal.

Grooming Table

A grooming table with a secure metal arm, a nylon loop with a safety release that goes around the dog's neck, and a comfortable surface are all additional grooming tools that will help during the process. Acclimate your dog gently to the grooming table, and never leave him unattended if he is on the table.

Nail Clippers and Files

For nail care, human nail clippers are adequate for puppy toenails. An adult Bernese Mountain Dog's nails will be thicker and tougher to clip, requiring a dog-specific nail clipper or an electric grinder. To file rough edges from your dog's nails, use a heavy metal nail file.

Scissors

In cold climates where ice and snow are normal, the hair between a Berner's pads can pick up ice balls or chemicals used to melt snow. Blunt-edged scissors are good to trim the hair from around a Berner's toes and between his pads. A neat foot is preferred by some owners. In addition, older dogs have more secure footing on slippery surfaces if the pads are trimmed.

Shampoo and Conditioner

Depending on the weather, a dog's activities, and the climate, a Bernese

Mountain Dog might need bathing twice a year or every six to eight weeks. Obviously, a Berner who has rolled around in the pasture muck might need more than just a spritz and a towel. Also, a dog with any skin condition may need more bathing or less, depending on the ailment. An extremely strong shampoo could exacerbate his skin condition or strip necessary protective oils from his skin and coat. A mild shampoo, followed by a thorough rinse with clear, cool water, will keep the Bernese Mountain Dog's coat shiny and silky. Puppies need a milder shampoo than grown Berners.

Shampoos and conditioners packaged in large jugs are handy for Berner owners with more than one dog. Consider buying products like this in bulk if your dogs have habits like lounging in the mud. Ask either your Berner's breeder or veterinarian for recommendations on shampoo type and frequency of baths.

In cold climates where ice and snow are normal, the hair between a Berner's pads can pick up ice balls or chemicals used to melt snow.

Identification

All Bernese Mountain dogs should have identification, including tags, as well as a permanent form of identification, such as a microchip or tattoo.

Tags

Your dog's tags should have basic contact information, including names and phone numbers of the owner and veterinary clinic. Many owners put their dog's name on the tag as well. However, a dog who responds to his name, even with strangers, can be a target of thieves.

Microchip

A microchip about the size of a grain of rice, is injected subcutaneously between the dog's shoulders. It is not a painful procedure. The chip contains a number unique to each dog, registered in a database. Some breeders microchip their Bernese Mountain Dog puppies before sending them off to their forever home. More than likely, your dog's veterinarian

BERNER NECESSITIES

- ✓ Purchase a big bed for a Bernese Mountain Dog.
- ✓ Buy a rolled leather collar, which won't snag a Berner's silky coat.
- ✓ Choose an extra-large crate for your large dog.
- ✓ Use stainless steel food and water bowls.
- ✓ Teach boundaries with a baby gate.
- ✓ Control shedding with a coat rake.
- ✓ Microchip your Bernese Mountain Dog and register the microchip number.
- ✓ Remember that leashes in 6- and 10-foot (2- and 3-m) lengths are good training aids.
- ✓ Supervise your Berner with his toys.
- ✓ Confine him with an exercise pen during travel or downtime.

will inject the microchip at the puppy's first visit. Dog at any age can be microchipped.

The dog's chip number, along with contact information that includes the names and phone numbers of the dog's owner and veterinarian, stays in the database. The cost to enroll a dog's microchip number is minimal. If the contact information needs to be changed or updated because the family has moved or changed their telephone number, these additions or deletions are easily done online.

The dog owner will receive a collar tag for her Berner with the dog's unique chip identification number, along with the microchip company's toll-free telephone number. A lost dog has a much better chance of being reunited with his owner if he has a chip.

So-called "universal scanners," available at most veterinary practices, are able to read any microchip if the scanning wand is waved above the dog's withers. Rarely, a chip will migrate to another area of the dog's body. For that reason, a test scan should be done at the dog's annual vet visit. If the chip has moved, a veterinarian can usually locate it; if not, inserting a replacement chip is a simple procedure.

Tattoo

Another permanent form of identification is a tattoo. Usually located in the dog's groin area or inside his earflap, tattoos have lost favor in the canine world. Microchips are simpler and don't inflict pain as tattooing a number right onto a dog's skin does.

Leash

Before you head off to explore the countryside, neighborhood, or park with your Bernese Mountain Dog, make sure that his leash is strong enough for a growing dog. Puppy leashes will get chewed, so don't spend a fortune on your Berner's first leash. He can learn to walk politely on an inexpensive cotton or nylon leash or even a piece of rope with a secure clasp tied to one end. As he grows, a Berner puppy can be taught to respect a nicer leather leash and not leave bite marks along its length.

Most puppy and dog manners classes, along with obedience classes, require that owners come prepared with a 6-foot (2-m) leash. As your dog becomes more proficient and begins to learn a *recall*, a long line from 10 feet (3 m) up to 30 feet (9 m) in length is an appropriate investment.

Toys

Dog toys range from very expensive toys that challenge a dog's thinking and reasoning skills to inexpensive cloth tugs. Because the Bernese Mountain Dog can be a powerful chewer and shredder, the best toy is one that comes with owner supervision. In other words, don't just leave toys out where your Berner has free access.

Some dog toys have holes through the middle for treats, peanut butter, bits of kibble, cheese, or other snacks to keep a dog entertained for up to a few hours.

Extreme chewers do well with toys that withstand harsh punishment, such as Nylabones.

Soft stuffed animals, sized appropriately for a growing Bernese Mountain Dog, can be used to teach beginning retrieving skills for a future obedience competitor. Bernese Mountain Dogs learn best through positive training methods, and some dogs prefer a favorite toy as a reward.

Be careful with any stuffed toy containing a squeaker, however. If a Berner puppy is a shredder, he might end up both with a squeaker and toy stuffing in his belly. Rope toys are dangerous for the same reason. Although a rope toy can provide valuable interaction time between a Berner and his owner, when tugging lessons end, the toy needs to be put away for the day.

If he is an extreme chewer, your Berner will do well with toys that withstand harsh punishment.

Chapter
4

Feeding Your
Bernese Mountain Dog

P roper nutrition is essential for a Bernese Mountain Dog. A hardworking breed, the content of his food is just as important as how much he eats.

Pet food and treat recalls justifiably frighten many dog owners. The best way to provide good nutrition to a Bernese Mountain Dog is to learn to read the labels on your dog's bag, pouch, or can of food. Know what goes into his food, whether it is dry kibble, canned, semi-moist, or even homemade.

A balanced diet helps a Berner grow, play, work, and enjoy his life. And many Berner owners know that the right diet and supplements will also add years to their dog's life.

All About Nutrition

Canine food must meet specific nutritional needs and include the necessary building blocks that are formulated for optimum health. These essential nutrients include carbohydrates, fats, minerals, proteins, vitamins, and especially, water.

Carbohydrates

Carbohydrates provide power to a dog in the form of energy. A Bernese Mountain Dog pulling a cart laden with 200 pounds

A hardworking breed, the content of your Berner's food is just as important as how much he eats.

(91 kg) off the start line does so with a burst of energy fueled by carbs. Examples of carbohydrates are starches, sugars, and fiber. These nutrients are digested in a dog's small intestines and then turned into glucose. Almost all of the cells in a dog's body are powered by glucose, but too much of a good thing is bad for a dog. Excess carbohydrates convert to fat.

In processed dog food, carbohydrate stores come from grains like wheat, rice, and corn. In some dog food, carbohydrates amount to more than 50 percent of the bulk. While processing improves the taste and digestibility of grains, some dogs are allergic to corn, oats, rice, barley, or wheat.

Dietary fiber carbohydrates in processed dog food usually come from soybean hulls, pea fiber, beet pulp, and bran from wheat, oats, or rice. Even though a dog can't digest fiber as easily as grains, fiber is still necessary for his intestines to function properly.

Fats

Most fats—which concentrate into increased energy for a dog—have been converted from carbohydrates. Fat is classified by its physical state, either saturated or unsaturated. Saturated fat is solid at room temperature, while unsaturated fat is liquid. Most dietary fat in dog food, however, is made up of triglycerides, basically a fatty acid chain;

Fatty acids promote a healthy skin and coat.

hence the term "essential fatty acid."

Fatty acids promote a healthy skin and coat and a strong immune system. But because essential fatty acids cannot be synthesized by a dog, these acids must be supplied in the diet.

Omega-6 and omega-3 fatty acids are the most-talked about supplements in canine nutrition. Many canine nutritionists and veterinarians have long recommended supplementing these two acids because they think that processed foods don't include nearly the adequate level for optimum health. Omega-6 acids occur in vegetable oils and animal fats.

DOG FOOD LABELS

The labels on prepackaged commercial dog foods detail the nutritional content of the food. Always read the label with your dog's specific needs in mind. For example, a slightly overweight Bernese Mountain Dog could be fed a kibble with a lower fat content. An active adult dog may need a kibble with both a higher fat and higher protein content. The protein source should be meat, and the better-quality kibbles will list the meat source first or second on the ingredient list. Avoid food that has a lot of grain sources, as these are frequently the cause of skin allergies in dogs. Also, keep in mind that the label might recommend 6 cups of food daily, while your dog will probably do well on 4 cups.

This triglyceride helps regulate blood flow throughout the dog's body and aids clotting after an injury. Omega-6 acids are important for optimum canine reproduction, to maintain healthy skin, and the Berner's long, silky coat, and to support a healthy immune system. Ongoing research in canine nutrition suggests that omega-3 fatty acids, derived from fish, are equally as important because they prevent inflammation in canines.

Fatty acid research has implications in the field of canine cancer prevention, an extremely urgent problem in the Bernese Mountain Dog community. It's believed that up to 60 percent of premature deaths in the breed are due to cancer.

Minerals

Minerals are pretty simple to keep track of compared to the fancy proteins, fats, and carbohydrates. Although balance is important and minerals must coordinate with other minerals to provide proper support, they also have to be available to the canine. Nutritionally, minerals help form the proper amount of cartilage and bone, they assist with the function of healthy muscles and nerves, and they help with oxygen transport. Minerals also maintain fluid balance, assist hormone production, and provide support to a canine's enzymes.

The so-called macro-minerals are calcium, phosphorus, sodium, chloride, potassium, and magnesium. Macro-minerals are required in greater amounts by the dog. Micro-minerals are added in trace amounts to dog food and include iron, zinc, copper, manganese, selenium, and iodine.

With all the work required of minerals, if the supplementation is incorrect, then a Berner can suffer health-wise. For example, an iodine imbalance could cause weight gain or a dull coat. Zinc insufficiency could lead to an increased number of infections.

Any suspected mineral deficiency should be evaluated by your Berner's veterinarian. The need for supplementation is incredibly difficult to evaluate based on either a hands-on or visual inspection; usually blood tests are required to determine if a dog suffers from a mineral imbalance.

Proteins

Protein is an essential nutrient that supports a canine's bodily functions. Dietary protein helps proper muscle and bone growth in a Bernese Mountain Dog puppy, while tissue repair requires protein as well. A Berner's immune system, which suppresses infections and inflammation, needs adequate protein, and his reproductive hormones are supplied in part from his dietary protein. The proteins in a Berner's diet also regulate enzyme production, which helps supply oxygen

A healthy diet will help give your Berner the energy he needs to get through the day.

transport throughout the dog's blood supply.

Proteins are the basic essential cellular building blocks, found in all animal and plant matter. Dietary proteins are digested by the dog to form amino acids, which then travel to the area of the dog's body that needs the most support. Because amino acids are not stored in a dog's body, they have to be provided in the diet. Also, because the dog has a constant need for amino acids, the protein in his food must be in the right quantity and of the highest quality.

A canine diet low in protein can lead to several health issues. These include decreased immune function, weight loss, a dull-looking coat, and a depressed appetite. Lactating bitches who don't receive the proper dietary protein, suffer a loss of milk production.

Conversely, a diet too rich in protein can cause weight gain, depending on the dog's lifestyle.

Trying to decipher the protein available in processed food by reading the label can get downright confusing. Most of your dog's food contains combinations of animal- and plant-sourced proteins, each of which provide different amino acids. In addition, dog food levels of protein are also calculated by the bioavailability, or how much of that protein is actually available to be used by a canine.

A canine diet low in protein can lead to decreased immune function, weight loss, a dull-looking coat, and a depressed appetite.

Puppy Love

FEEDING YOUR BERNER PUPPY

Your puppy's breeder should recommend the type of food she has been feeding her Berner brood. To prevent any stomach upsets, especially while your pup is getting used to his new home, try to feed the same food on the same schedule. The quality of the food is extremely important to a Bernese Mountain Dog puppy. If his nutrition is incomplete or unbalanced, his growth could be stunted and never regained. A Bernese Mountain Dog puppy's physical development continues through the first year of his life, so plan to keep your dog on a complete, quality, lower-protein food during this phase of rapid growth.

In most dog food, protein comes from meat or meat by-products. In a high-end dog food, the protein source will be listed as the first or second ingredient on the label. The source should also identify whether the protein is from animal or plant matter.

Because the Bernese Mountain Dog is large-boned, a low or moderately low protein diet is recommended. Rapid bone growth should be discouraged because a growing puppy's muscles and tendons cannot support such fast growth. For a Bernese Mountain Dog, slow and steady is definitely better when it comes to growth.

Vitamins

Vitamins, compared to other nutrients, impact the work of all the proteins, fats, and minerals in a dog's diet. Vitamins are only needed in small amounts, however.

Vitamins are either fat-soluble or water-soluble. Vitamins A, D, E, and K cannot be used by a dog unless he has enough dietary fat. Likewise, the water-soluble vitamins B and C can only be utilized if he receives enough water.

Normal vision, growth, immune function, and reproduction are all helped by adequate amounts of vitamin A. This vitamin is an antioxidant, which means that it contains important anti-cancer and anti-inflammatory properties. Usually vitamin A is added to a dog's food from a plant source such as carrots. Vitamin D, a calcium regulator, helps a dog grow strong bones. The antioxidant vitamin E plays a role in reproduction. Sources include safflower, soybean oil, and wheat germ. Green, leafy plants and vegetable sources provide vitamin K, which helps blood to clot after an injury.

Water-soluble B complex vitamins are critical for the metabolism of proteins, carbohydrates, and fats and are the workhorses of energy for dogs. Because dogs make their own vitamin C, this does not need to be added to their diet unless advised by a veterinarian or canine nutritionist.

Water

Water is so important to a dog that any deviation—high or low—has an adverse effect on him.

None of the essential nutrients works properly if dogs don't have a good base of available water. Whether a dog laps it up from his bucket, or it is mixed into the feed, or it is generated from metabolic processes in a Berner's body, adequate stores of water help him regulate body temperature, lubricate his joints and tissues, and give his blood cells the medium to ride along the vascular system.

Adequate stores of water help the Berner regulate body temperature, lubricate his joints and tissues, and give his blood cells the medium to ride along the vascular system.

A Bernese Mountain Dog's daily water requirement is decided by his activity level and his food amount. If a dog eats more, he will drink more. If he eats a water-based canned or moist food, he won't need to drink as much. Pregnant or lactating bitches need more water than most dogs, as do Berners who work hard on a farm. Your Berner should always have access to cool, clean water unless otherwise instructed by your veterinarian.

Feeding Schedule

Your Berner should be put on a feeding schedule that does not change unless he is ill or his activity level changes.

Free-feeding a Berner, or leaving food out all day for him to pick over at will, may be convenient for you but is not healthy for your dog for a couple of reasons. If you have a multi-dog household, you will never know if one dog is getting too much food or not enough if all the food is placed out for them to graze at will during the day. In addition, free-feeding leads to weight gain. A regular feeding schedule is much healthier and better overall for your Bernese Mountain Dog.

Types of Food

Given all the nutrients essential for a healthy Bernese Mountain Dog, the type and amount of food is more important with regard to this breed than for almost any

For optimum health, put your Berner on a feeding schedule.

other breed of dog. A Berner needs a very high-quality food—not junk food—because cancer often kills this breed. Many fanciers are adamant that the better the food, the healthier the Berner. There is quite a lot of science to back up their claims.

Keep in mind that just because a dog food comes in a bag doesn't make it a low-quality food. Conversely, a home-cooked diet can contain all the right things for a Berner, but if the proportions of nutrients are off, the dog can become sick.

So with all the types of diets available,

how does a conscientious owner decide what to feed her Berner? The best type of diet is the one that works for you and your dog. If your Berner is thriving, his coat is shiny, his skin and eyes are clear, his joints don't ache, and he's energetic and happy, then his diet is probably just fine. But if your Bernese Mountain Dog suffers from allergies, is obese, or is failing to thrive, a diet consultation with a certified nutritionist or a veterinarian schooled in canine nutrition should be considered.

A low-protein food is recommended for a Bernese Mountain Dog puppy so that his bones are not strained by too-rapid growth. He might eat up to 2 cups of food three times a day. An adult Bernese Mountain Dog might, based on his activity level, need 2 cups of food twice daily.

Deciding on the right diet should not make you anxious. The choices can be confusing and overwhelming at times, but you can make the best dog food decision if you are educated.

Commercial Foods

Dog food that is pre-packaged, processed, nutritionally complete, and readily available to consumers is considered "commercial." Commercial foods come dry, semi-moist, and canned.

Dry Food (Kibble)

Dry food is bagged, processed, and hardened into a kibble that is palatable to the dog and convenient for his owner to store and dispense. Dry kibble also contains additives to maintain the taste, texture, and shelf life, and to restore nutrients destroyed in the manufacturing process.

Dry food stays fresher longer, which adds to the convenience. Because Berners need a very high-quality kibble, which is usually more expensive than many brands, the costs can add up, but the better the food, the healthier the dog, and the more active

he can remain. Bulk purchases of dry food are more economical.

Proactive Bernese Mountain Dog owners read the labels on dog food. The ingredients are listed by weight in descending order; higher-quality food lists meat as the main protein source. A grain-based protein source may not make the best kibble for a Berner because dogs don't digest grains as well as they do meats.

If the label defines the protein source, all the better. Rather than the generic word "meat," look for food that states what kind of meat, such as chicken or lamb. The label should also list other additions, like blueberries, which add nutrients. The fewer ingredients on the label, the better the food. Fewer ingredients means that your Berner will be less likely to develop a food allergy or be subjected to extra chemicals that are not good for him.

Dry food is bagged, processed, and hardened into a kibble that is palatable to the dog and convenient for his owner to store and dispense.

A QUALITY BERNESE DIET

Q: What do you feed your Bernese Mountain Dogs?

A: "Some breeders feed all raw; we use very high-quality moist food. It's not just the type of dog food that's important—we also supplement their diet with fresh, pureed veggies like broccoli once a week. We rotate that with sardines and yogurt. These make sure that the dogs get probiotics to help their coats and digestive tracts."

—Sloane Shepard, Bernese Mountain Dog Club of America
(BMDCA) regional rescue coordinator

Semi-Moist Food

Semi-moist food usually tastes better to a dog: He might jump up and think, "Oh yea! Hamburger for dinner!" The food is in smaller packets, is easy to store in a pantry, and is convenient. Semi-moist food also contains water, so a Berner might not drink as much from his water bowl.

However, the convenience of semi-moist food comes with a price. These foods have a shorter shelf life and contain large amounts of preservatives. Semi-moist dog food also contains a high amount of sugar to increase palatability, which in turn, causes weight gain in less active dogs. Berners, especially, tend to gain extra weight, so a semi-moist food is not the best option for this breed.

Canned Food

Canned food may be convenient and palatable, but it is almost 75 percent water. An opened can cannot be stored for long because bacterial growth begins almost immediately after the can is opened. Any opened, unused can of dog food should be thrown away after two or three days.

Noncommercial Foods

Many Bernese Mountain Dog fanciers have turned to noncommercial foods for their dogs, whether home-cooked diet or raw, or a combination of the two, along with some commercially prepared food.

Noncommercial food must be carefully managed and must contain the proper nutrients in the correct amounts and ratios. These special diets are much more time-consuming to prepare, cost more money, and unless they are prepared with the advice of a canine nutrition specialist, your dog could become deficient in one or more essential dietary nutrients.

That said, because cancer and other inflammation-based diseases are seen overwhelmingly in Bernese Mountain Dogs, noncommercial foods are considered much healthier and appropriate for this breed. Keep in mind, however, that home-cooked or raw diets aren't appropriate for a Bernese Mountain Dog who has an immune dysfunction unless there is direct involvement and advice from a veterinarian or nutritionist.

If the dog owner or any immediate family member has a compromised immune system, feeding a raw diet to a dog can expose the family to harmful bacteria or parasites.

Also, if the dog owner or any immediate family member has a compromised immune system, feeding a raw diet to a dog can expose the family to harmful bacteria or parasites. The Centers for Disease Control and Prevention (CDC) and the Food and Drug Administration (FDA) have guidelines on their respective websites about the use of raw or home-cooked dog food.

Home-Cooked Diet

A home-prepared diet gives the Berner owner control over what goes into her dog's food. Recipes are available online and in some excellent printed resources. The recipes allow for a variety of meats, vegetables, and grains. Some home-cookers will slowly change their dog's diet over by adding freshly cooked meat and vegetables to his kibble. And meals can be prepared in advance and stored in the freezer.

Don't just throw some meat into a stockpot and add veggies, however. Stick with proven recipes, and add the required supplements—vitamins and minerals—that your Berner needs to stay healthy.

Raw Diet

A raw diet is just what it sounds like: all raw vegetables and meat. Some raw diet advocates avoid grains; others suggest adding cooked rice to raw meat. A raw diet is not hard to prepare, but it must be supplemented with the proper vitamins and minerals in the proper proportions. Because fresh foods are more expensive, a raw diet, likewise, is more expensive than commercially prepared dog food.

Raw, meaty bones obtained from a reputable butcher are excellent treats for Bernese Mountain Dogs. Once a Berner has sucked out all the marrow and eaten the meat, he can chew on the marrow bone for hours or days. These bones can also be flash-frozen, stuffed with peanut butter, cheese, and dry kibble, and continue to provide entertainment and nourishment while he's in his crate or exercise pen. Raw bones can even be ground up and added to your dog's bowl. That way, his consumption of raw bones will be supervised and safe.

Small, soft, cooked bones are dangerous for any dog and should never be given to a Bernese Mountain Dog. They can splinter and lodge in his mouth, throat, or stomach, which can precipitate a gastrointestinal crisis or surgery.

There are some common sense precautions related to feeding a raw diet to your Berner. Only buy meat that has been inspected and declared free of parasites. Purchase meat from a reputable butcher or grocery store. Don't leave raw meat in your car while you run all the other errands you have on that day. To prevent cross-contamination with

Raw, meaty bones obtained from a reputable butcher are excellent treats for Bernese Mountain Dogs.

Salmonella, *E. coli*, and other organisms present in raw foods that can cause disease in dogs and humans, always clean countertops, chopping boards, and cooking utensils before and after raw food preparation.

The Obesity Epidemic

Just as human health is negatively impacted by obesity, so too is canine health. The obesity epidemic endangers a dog's well-being in some of the same ways that it affects his owner. Extreme stress on bones and joints leads to orthopedic injuries. A heavy layer of fat hurts heart, lung, and kidney function. An obese dog cannot exercise as much as he should. Also, obesity shortens a dog's life. In Bernese Mountain Dogs, with an already too-short life expectancy, the consequence of obesity is tragic.

A dog is considered too heavy if you cannot feel his ribs beneath his coat or if you cannot see a waistline when you

The best methods to combat obesity are increased exercise and reduced calories.

Check It Out

FEEDING FACTS

✓ Feed your Berner a high-quality food.

✓ Essential nutrients include carbohydrates, fats, minerals, proteins, and vitamins.

✓ Feed meat-sourced proteins.

✓ Carbs and fats provide your dog with energy. Vitamins and minerals help the immune system.

✓ Adult Berners eat about 4 cups of food daily.

✓ Dry kibble is economical for this large breed; semi-moist food tastes great to dogs but is usually full of sugar and preservatives; and canned food is mostly water, so you have to feed more to fill up your Berner.

✓ Home-cooked and raw diets are preservative-free.

✓ Carefully balance the nutritional requirements in home-cooked dog food. Imbalanced food leads to canine illness.

✓ Feed a puppy three or four times daily; feed an adult Berner twice each day.

✓ Free-feeding leads to obesity—a regular feeding schedule is much healthier for your dog.

✓ Obese dogs suffer heart, lung, kidney, and joint disease.

look at him from above. Don't mistake the lack of a tuck-up at the dog's groin (when looked at from the side) as a sign of obesity. Bernese Mountain Dogs do not have a generous tuck in front of their stifle. Rather, put your hands on your dog. Have your vet weigh him on a regular basis. Watch for signs of weight gain, which may take the form of orthopedic issues like sore joints after a leisurely walk.

The best methods to combat obesity are increased exercise and reduced calories. Watch the amount and types of treats that you give to your dog, and cut back his food intake. If your Berner looks at you as if he's starving, add 1/2 cup of fresh green beans to his kibble. Rather than giving high-calorie treats, substitute lower-calorie veggies, such as pieces of carrot. Don't feed table scraps, especially human food high in carbohydrates.

A Bernese Mountain Dog who seems unable to lose extra pounds (kg) should have a thorough evaluation by his veterinarian. Some clinical conditions can cause canine obesity, so a checkup is warranted.

Chapter
5

Grooming Your Bernese Mountain Dog

A Bernese Mountain Dog's beautiful coat deserves special care to keep him looking his best. A daily brushing regimen is easy to incorporate into even a busy owner's life. A few minutes of maintenance grooming every day can prevent mat development. Overlooking this daily grooming need can lead to a difficult grooming job within a few weeks.

Grooming Supplies

You will need the following grooming supplies to keep your Berner looking his best:

- **brush:** either steel or hardy bristle coat brush
- **coat rake:** de-shedder or wide-tined metal loop to remove dead undercoat
- **conditioner:** if needed to keep coat silky
- **cotton balls:** use during bathing to protect ear canal
- **ear cleaner:** foaming solution to clean ears, and drying solution

The Berner's thick double coat sheds quite a bit.

- **eye wash:** water-based eye drops to clear small debris from eyes
- **grooming table with arm and neck loop:** sturdy table for ease in grooming dog for the conformation ring
- **hair dryer:** high-velocity canine-specific forced air-dryer
- **nail file, heavy duty:** either dog specific or human-use grade
- **nail trimmer:** either clipper or grinder to keep nails short
- **scissors:** blunt edged to trim hair around paw and between pads

A wide-tined metal loop will help remove dead undercoat.

- **shampoo:** keeps coat and skin clean
- **soft damp cloth:** microfiber or cotton cloth to control "flyaways" and reduce allergens
- **stainless steel comb:** wide-toothed comb for keeping ear feathers neat
- **styptic powder or paste:** used to stop bleeding if nail quick is clipped
- **toothbrush or finger brush:** canine specific to apply toothpaste
- **toothpaste:** specific for dogs, usually peanut butter or meat flavored

Brushing and Combing

A Bernese Mountain Dog sheds. Anyone thinking about this breed needs to understand that while regular grooming will keep more of the shed coat in the trash and not floating in clouds throughout the home, your dog's thick double coat is still going to shed year-round. Nothing will prevent that.

With that said, regular coat brushing and combing will help manage your dog's beautiful thick, silky fur. Daily brushing is the single best grooming regimen a Berner owner can perform to keep his coat in excellent condition. If the coat becomes too tangled to comb, especially the fine feathering around the dog's ears or underneath his tail, then mats might need to be clipped or scissored out of the coat.

How to Do It

Brushing the coat should begin with an inspection of the feathers along the dog's ears, beneath his tail, and on his thighs.

GROOMING AS A HEALTH CHECK

Grooming day, in addition to quality bonding time between you and your Bernese Mountain Dog, is also the perfect opportunity to conduct needed health checks. An unexpected tick can be found by doing a hands-on rubdown. Flea infestations can be averted by watching for the signs—tiny brown or black flecks left on the table or caught between the tines of a comb. Your touch can detect odd lumps or growths that might be early signs of cancerous growth. Use all your senses to check out your dog's health. Do you see cloudiness in your dog's eyes? Do you smell yeast in his ears? Do your fingers feel a lump that you didn't detect during your dog's previous bath? Is his skin dry? Don't reserve your dog's regular grooming just for those chores to help him look and smell his best. Every grooming session is an opportunity to maintain your canine's health.

Gently comb the feathers with a wide-toothed steel comb. Work out any mats with slight pressure. If the mats are thick, consider cutting the hair away using blunt or round-tipped scissors. Always point scissors away from the dog's body in case he jerks.

Use a coat rake to loosen and pull the dead undercoat away from the dog. Always rake in the same direction as the coat growth so that the dog's hair is not pulled out by the follicles. Get the rake deep into the double undercoat and pull firmly and with a long, steady stroke.

Unless your Berner is destined for the conformation ring, consider using one of the de-shedding tools on the market. A de-shedder loosens thick fur, but it can also cut healthy fur during a shed. If you are preparing your Berner for the show ring, a de-shedder can harm his coat. But for the Berner who participates in other canine sports or who is a homebody, a de-shedder can help speed up the heaviest shed period. As with a rake, always use firm strokes in the direction of the coat growth. Stroke up and away from your dog's body. Because some of these types of grooming tools have a sharp blade, be very careful not to accidentally nick your dog's skin.

Follow the rake and de-shedder with a good all-purpose natural bristle brush. Stroke firmly in the direction of hair growth, and don't forget the chest, neck, and head. A bristle brush should be firm enough that the bristles attract and collect loose fur but not so firm that brushing tickles or irritates your Berner's tender skin. Your Bernese Mountain Dog might enjoy lying down for a final brush of his belly.

After the raking, de-shedding, and brushing, use either a hand glove or soft towel to finish, which will give your dog's coat a healthy, shiny glow. A hand mitt might have a smooth side and a dimpled side. Slightly moisten the cloth or mitt, and rub your Berner's coat from nose to tail. A good rubdown with a soft, barely damp cloth will also help reduce pollen or other allergens that your dog might bring in from his outside strolls.

By putting your hands on your dog after his grooming ritual, you can notice any

Use a coat rake to loosen and pull the dead undercoat away from the dog.

THE GROOMING TABLE

Puppies easily adapt to the use of a grooming table if the owner takes the time to make the session a game. If possible, use a table with legs that can be lowered so that a fearful puppy isn't frightened by an extreme height. With the table lowered almost to the ground, let your puppy clamber up and around the table. Put a towel on the table to provide more traction.

Over several weeks, your puppy will develop a tolerance for the grooming table if you always give him praise while he sits quietly on top of the table. Pair his willingness to stand quietly on the table with a very tasty treat. As he acclimates to the grooming table, begin to perform grooming tasks while he is sitting the table, then standing, then lying down.

Patience, good humor, and a pocketful of healthy treats will help your Berner pup look forward to his table time.

tangles or mats unintentionally missed. More important, though, this is the time during grooming that you can notice any unusual sores, lumps, bumps, or hotspots. Because his coat is so thick, also take the opportunity to look for ticks or evidence of flea infestation.

Bathing

Depending on his living and working circumstances, a Berner might need to be bathed every couple of months or only twice a year. If he takes on that "doggy" smell, he needs a bath. If he has fleas or another skin condition, he might need to be bathed with medicated shampoo. A working Berner might not need a bath as often as a conformation show ring Berner does.

How to Do It

Teach your Berner to stand in a tub (either outside or inside) with encouragement and treats. Let him become accustomed to water splashing on his feet, then his legs, and then his back, and tell him constantly that he is a brave Berner indeed.

When he is comfortable standing in the tub and he accepts the spray from a shower or hose, put cotton balls in his ears to protect the canals. Then wet his thick coat thoroughly, from head to tail. Starting at his head, squirt the shampoo along his back, legs, and his sides and into his tail. Massage the shampoo into his coat gently, taking special care not to get soap in his eyes. To clean his head and face, use a soft, soapy cloth. Don't neglect

Depending on his living and working circumstances, a Berner might need to be bathed every couple of months or only twice a year.

dry; others use high-powered forced air blowers, which use cool or slightly warm air to blow-dry the dog's coat.

Dental Care

Dental care is one of the most proactive things a Berner owner can do to keep her dog healthy. Plaque and tartar can lead to periodontal disease, and bacteria in the mouth resulting from this condition can move through the bloodstream and contribute to heart, liver, and kidney disease.

Veterinarians report that by the time a dog is three or four years old, he'll have some evidence of dental disease. He could have a buildup of tartar, especially on the rear molars, or his gums could be inflamed and begin to recede from the base of his teeth. Dogs crack their teeth when they chew on marrow bones, sticks, or rocks. Oral abscesses can require a root canal if the infection isn't caught early. Dogs can even get splinters in their gums when they play tug-of-war with sticks.

Daily brushing and oral inspections can head off major problems down the road, as well as help improve your Bernese Mountain Dog's overall health.

his belly. Talk quietly to your dog during his bath, and offer praise and bits of treats when he cooperates.

Rinsing the shampoo out of the dog's coat should take twice the time it took you to lather him up. Begin at his head, and use either your hands or a soft brush to squeeze the soap out of his coat. Rinse until no more soap runs off the dog.

A Berner will likely shake vigorously when he exits the tub, so prepare to get wet. Have plenty of thick towels available to wring the water out of his coat—and off of yourself. Some owners let their dog air-

How to Do It

Canine-specific toothpaste comes flavored to make it more palatable to dogs. Never use human-grade toothpaste, as some of the chemicals can make a dog nauseated or ill.

Begin slowly to acclimate your dog to the toothpaste. Put a tiny amount on your fingertip and let him lick it. Then put a dab on either a canine toothbrush or on a fingertip brush, which you slide over the end of your index finger. Let the dog lick the brush. Next, put another small amount of paste on the brush and begin at the dog's back molars. If he won't let you put the brush on more than one tooth, tell him how brave he is and put the supplies away. He will work the toothpaste around in his mouth and swallow. The next day, try again. Over a week or two, your dog should allow you to brush all of his teeth. If he objects to the toothbrush, then switch to the fingertip brush.

Some canine toys and treats claim to help keep a dog's teeth healthy. Some of the hype is marketing, but some items actually can maintain your Berner's oral health. Raw meaty soup bones are hard enough that a dog can chew on the bone for days, and in the process, reduce any deposits on his teeth. Hard knobby plastic toys, such as those made by Nylabone, can also help, but you should always supervise your Berner while he's chewing on them.

Ear Care

Ear care is just as important as coat care for the Bernese Mountain Dog. Berners who work on farms or track in brush and woods can pick up dust and debris that lodge in the ear canal. In multiple-dog homes, Bernese Mountain Dogs play "kissy kissy" and lick each other's ears, and the moisture sets up fungal and bacterial infections. Also, if the moisture is not dried from a Berner's ear canals after a bath, those same infections can fester. The ears are also ripe for mite infestations.

A well-groomed Bernese Mountain Dog is a joy to behold.

A TYPICAL GROOMING SESSION

Q: What is a typical grooming session for a Bernese Mountain Dog?

A: "Brush the coat daily because if you don't, they're going to get mats. I bathe every six weeks and check the ears all the time. The hair growth between the pads can get very thick, so I clip the fur to give the dog better house traction. And new owners are shocked at the amount of hair shed by a Bernese Mountain Dog. You haven't cooked your food right unless you find a little Berner hair in it."

—Sloane Shepard, Bernese Mountain Dog Club of America
(BMDCA) regional rescue coordinator

How to Do It

Ear checks on a weekly basis can help prevent these illnesses, which can be quite painful to a dog. If a problem is detected early, treatment is easier and less expensive.

A number of over-the-counter and prescriptions products are available to clean your Berner's ears. Clean the ears outside the house if possible because your dog will fling his head from side to side, and the cleaner will fly.

First, use a foaming liquid that loosens the dirt and earwax. Tilt the dog's head to one side and hold his collar. Squirt a small amount of the cleaner into his ear canal. Never force the nozzle down into the canal, as this could damage the ear. Rub the base of the ear gently, and allow the foaming action to do the job of cleaning the canal. Do this with both ears.

Follow the foaming cleaner with a drying agent, which will help the liquid evaporate. Most of these types of agents have small amounts of rubbing alcohol in the ingredients. If your dog's ears have any small scratches, keep in mind that this could sting. Hold your dog's collar firmly as you squirt the drying agent into the canal of each ear. Again, gently rub the base of the ear so that the liquid descends into the ear canal.

Finally, take a cotton ball or soft cloth and clean any grime or dirt that you can see on the inside ear flap. Never insert a cotton swab into your dog's ear. Because a dog's ear canal is angled, a swab can easily break off and damage his eardrum.

If you notice evidence of ear mites, which look like coffee grounds, or if your dog's ears have a yeast-like smell, have your veterinarian evaluate him for infection or infestation.

Eye Care

Eye care is equally important for a Bernese Mountain Dog. His big, beautiful brown eyes deserve attention, and not just when he's asking to climb into your lap.

How to Do It

During the weekly grooming session, pay close attention to his eyes. Bernese Mountain Dogs are known to suffer from the conditions entropion and ectropion. Entropion causes a dog's eyelids to roll inward. Every time the dog opens and closes his eyes, the lashes rub against his corneas. This is a painful condition that causes increased tear production, and it can lead to chronic eye inflammation. If it's not corrected, the dog can become blind. If you notice increased tears or inflamed eye tissue, get a veterinary ophthalmologist to evaluate the dog. Surgery is necessary to correct entropion.

Ectropion causes a dog's eyelids to be too loose. Typically, the lower lid will sag and not just when the dog is tired after a long day of play and activity. The lid rolls outward and doesn't protect his eye from dust or debris. Chronic inflammation can result from ectropion, but surgery—a type of canine "eyelift"—will correct the condition.

A Bernese Mountain Dog who has been working on a field or farm can pick up debris, from dust to small seed grains, that lodges in his eyes. Human-grade, preservative-free eye drops or artificial tears can be used to flush his eyes. If the dirt is lodged and cannot be removed with a flushing agent, take your dog to his veterinarian right away. Even specks of sand can scratch his cornea.

Foot and Nail Care

To keep a Berner's feet in good condition, the feet and nails should be inspected weekly and the pad hair and nails trimmed

A Bernese Mountain Dog who has been working on a field or farm can pick up debris, from dust to small seed grains, that lodges in his eyes.

when necessary. If your dog lives in a harsh winter climate, painful ice balls can form between the pads, or he could be walking through ice and snow-melting chemicals. Hair between the pads can cause a dog to slip on tile or hardwood floors.

If your dog's footfall causes a loud, audible "click" on a tile or hardwood floor or on the street when walking, then the nails should be trimmed. Nails that are too long can cause the dog's feet to splay or the toes to spread too far apart. Either a nail grinder or a clipper will work, but if a grinder is used, be very careful not to grab any of the hair either around the nails or between the pads. Not only can this frighten your dog, but it can be quite painful and rip out patches of fur. Done properly, a grinder can be the fastest and easiest way to trim a dog's nails.

How to Do It

Use a damp cloth to clean between your dog's pads. If the hair seems long, use blunt-edged scissors to trim the hair level with the pads. Some owners also neaten up the hair around the nails, just to give the feet a clean appearance. If your dog has any sores or scratches on his pads, clean them with soapy lukewarm water. Keep an eye on any open sores on the pads, and always get a veterinary evaluation for any open wound that looks deep or oozes.

Acclimate a Berner puppy to nail trimming slowly and the process will be easier for all involved. From his first day at his new home, your pup should have his toes and feet handled at least daily. Pair foot handling with a smile, kind words, and bits of treats so that by the time his nails need to be trimmed, he will associate good things with his feet being touched.

If using a grinder, acclimate your dog to the sound first before attempting to grind the nails. With the grinder turned on, let your dog investigate the noise without getting too close to the drum. Tell him what a brave boy he is,

Dogs who walk on pavement often wear their nails down naturally and so may not need trims as often.

Check It Out

GROOMING CHECKLIST

✓ Bernese Mountain Dogs shed.
✓ Brush a Berner daily to control shedding and prevent mats.
✓ Clip mats with blunt-edged scissors.
✓ Comb ear and leg feathers.
✓ Bathe about every six weeks to every six months or when necessary.
✓ Dry the dog thoroughly.
✓ Wipe him with a soft damp cloth to increase coat shine.

✓ Trim the hair between the pads and around his toes.
✓ Clip or grind the nails monthly.
✓ Inspect the ears daily and clean them weekly.
✓ Check the eyes daily and flush debris with eyewash.
✓ Brush the teeth daily.

give him a special treat, and turn it off.

The first time a grinder is used on your dog's nails, trim one nail, treat and praise, and stop. Later, grind another nail, treat, and stop. Touch the drum to each nail for no longer than two or three seconds. It's not necessary to apply pressure to the nail because the speed of the grinder along with the sanding band does all the work. The same process applies with a pair of nail clippers. Simply acclimate your puppy to the touch of the tool before actually cutting a nail. Cut just the tip of the nail, then praise and offer a tasty treat to the dog. Go slowly to protect the quick from accidental clipping.

Because some or all of a Berner's toenails are black, the nail quick—the blood vessel running through the nail—can be tricky to see. The quick might be visible as either a white, silver, or pale pink sliver under the nail. If you accidentally nick the quick using either a grinder or clipper, press the nail in styptic power to staunch the bleeding. If you're like a lot of owners, the first time you nick the quick, the nail bleeds, and your dog winces, you'll vow to always take him to a groomer or veterinary technician for all subsequent nail trims. That's okay too. Your Bernese Mountain Dog will appreciate the car ride and camaraderie with you.

Some groomers file down rough nail edges with a sturdy metal dog- or human-grade steel nail file. This protects carpet and furniture from snags due to sharp nail edges. With firm pressure, swipe the nail in one direction to remove any sharp edge.

Chapter 6

Training Your
Bernese Mountain Dog

From the moment a Bernese Mountain Dog puppy or adult goes to his forever home, he will love his owners unconditionally. Reciprocally, his owners have an obligation to house, feed, and love him right back. Berner owners also have a responsibility to train their dogs.

Unlike some much smaller breeds that can be tucked in a handbag or stroller, a Bernese Mountain Dog is going to be noticed. Because a Berner is so big and because he is so beautiful, his owner will hear comments and questions from the public: "He's so huge!" "He's so pretty!" "How much does he eat?" "Where does he sleep?"

A Bernese Mountain Dog owner who hears, "Wow, he is so well behaved! How did you train him to mind you?" is the owner whom the Berner deserves. A Berner owner has a moral obligation to teach the dog how to behave, and not just for his safety. Enactment of breed-specific legislation often targets large dogs. While large- and giant-breed dogs, statistically, are not the most dangerous in terms of bites to humans or dog-on-dog attacks, they are often the dogs who are cited by the public as being threats, although the Bernese Mountain Dog is typically gentle.

Because he is so beautiful and because he is so large, a Berner who misbehaves in public or in his home will leave a much larger negative impression. Likewise, the owner who understands that her Berner requires training and socialization to integrate well, both in the house and in society, does a service to all big dogs. Large dogs require that level of responsibility from their owners.

A dog who behaves in public, minds the house manners and rules, and even participates in canine sports is a happier dog. The Berner who knows and understands commands, as simple as *sit* and *stay,* is the dog who is unlikely to end

A dog who behaves in public, minds the house manners and rules, and even participates in canine sports is a happier dog.

up in a rescue or shelter. A dog who responds to commands to *come* or *heel,* will participate more fully in his owner's life. This is the Berner who is a joy to have around, a joy to live with, and a joy to take out in public.

Positive Training

By the time your Berner has reached his first birthday, his bad habits should be minimized, his good manners reinforced, and his ability to follow directions praised, but training a Berner is especially fraught with potential pitfalls because these are sensitive dogs who are aloof and can be shy. A Bernese Mountain Dog won't work for hours to perfect a behavior like some of the retrievers will do.

Something as simple as praise for a job well done is an example of a reward.

What Positive Training Entails

Positive training works best with this smart, sensitive breed, not a heavy hand. The keys to successful positive training are patience, a sense of humor, a bag of treats as rewards, and a clicker to mark a desired behavior. A clicker is a small, simple device that sounds like a cricket, although some trainers use a verbal marker, such as "yes!", to let the dog know that he's correct. It doesn't matter which method is used as long as the dog understands.

Positive training doesn't mean that a dog never hears the word "no." Positive trainers might use a variety of methods to help a dog learn, short of aversives, like a prong or electric collar. Even so, just as individuals differ, so do dogs, each displaying unique personalities. Some Berners, especially adolescents or older dogs who have had no prior training, might need a different approach. The best trainers will only use the tools that the individual dog requires to help him learn—no more and no less.

PUPPY SOCIALIZATION

A good puppy kindergarten and socialization class offers a balance of play and interaction for puppies. Formal lessons are incorporated into the play. A shy Berner benefits from all experiences in socialization, which help him grow up to be confident and bold.

Loading the Clicker

Before trying to train your dog with a clicker and treats, first "load" the clicker with a generous supply of treats or kibble as rewards. Every time he looks at your face, either click or say "yes," and immediately feed him a few pieces of kibble or a treat. Do this in rapid-fire succession until you've given him 10 to 20 pieces of treats.

Now your smart little puppy knows that every time he hears the click or your voice saying "yes," he will get a reward. He has realized that when he looks at your face, he can "force" you to say the magic word and then give him a treat. Quite probably, he believes that he has just trained you.

You can break down large treats into smaller pieces as rewards for your Berner.

This critical first step should not be neglected, or else your dog will not understand all of the positive training methods that will follow. You have just taught him that when he looks to you for information or guidance, you will let him know if he is correct and that you appreciate his efforts by rewarding him.

The Secret of Positive Training

That is pretty much the "secret" of positive training: Information leads to behavior, which leads to rewards. Along the way, the amount of information (training) given to your Berner will increase or vary; he will offer the behavior based on the information given ("stay"); and then, because he did what he was told, he will be rewarded, sometimes immediately with a treat, or a little later, during play with you and a favorite tug toy.

Socialization

At the same time that training a Bernese Mountain Dog puppy begins, he must also be introduced to other people, dogs, situations, and environments. This critical period of socialization is crucial, and for the Berner, a vital part of his education. Because these dogs are bred to be aloof and reserved, shyness has also cropped up as a breed tendency. Strangers can be scary, children too loud, other dogs too intimidating, and traffic too noisy. Proper socialization can help a puppy overcome his shyness or fear and help him become comfortable in most situations. A well-adapted dog doesn't just grow up—he needs nurturing and guidance along the way.

With Dogs

Puppy kindergarten, a sort of puppy play date paired with short training sessions, will help a Berner pup grow into a confident adult dog. Typically, puppy-K might be a 45-minute session for youngsters under six months of age. Puppies are encouraged to interact with other puppies of different sizes and appearances. Also, the owners of the puppies handle each dog in the class for a short time. A "pass the puppy" game involves each puppy and his owner sitting on the floor, with the dogs passed in a

Prior to attending any group training classes, but especially puppy classes, make sure that your Bernese Mountain Dog pup is fully vaccinated for his age and his activities.

clockwise circle until each puppy has been petted and touched by all the other owners.

This scenario isn't popular with all puppy trainers or owners. A fearful puppy could feel even less in control of his situation. If your puppy shows any signs of a "puppy meltdown"—if he begins to claw and scratch to get back to his owner, if he urinates or defecates submissively, or if his hackles are raised by a more dominant pup—end the game. Let him sit on the sidelines at first to just watch. He might need to sniff his surroundings before joining in any puppy games.

At some point, either because you need to hand him off or because he's decided to be bold, your puppy should show interest in other dogs at a puppy kindergarten. Continue to reassure him that he is the bravest little big dog.

Prior to attending any group training classes, but especially puppy classes, make sure that your Bernese Mountain Dog pup is fully vaccinated for his age and his activities. Most training centers, grooming shops, and boarding facilities will require this to protect all of the client dogs from communicable diseases. If your puppy isn't fully vaccinated but you want to begin his socialization, take him places where you know that the adult dogs are healthy. For example, find a neighbor with well-behaved dogs where you can take your puppy on a visit.

With Children

Older children and young tweens are ideal puppy socializers. Never leave children and puppies unattended, but do encourage them to play and cuddle. Young Bernese Mountain Dogs, despite their large-breed status, are fragile. Don't let your own children bully or tease any puppy because some puppies don't have very good bite inhibition.

If your Berner is shy or fearful around other dogs, make introductions slowly and carefully.

LISTEN TO YOUR BERNER

Q: How do you get your Berner to learn commands?

A: "The more you listen to the dog, the more the dog will respond to you."

—Kim K. Kirkpatrick, owner/trainer/handler

A Bernese Mountain Dog puppy can act terribly stubborn at times. The pup might not want to give his toy back to a child, and a tug-of-war may ensue. The puppy needs to be taught that he cannot snap at any human skin but especially a child's, just to retrieve a toy. Likewise, children in the home must be taught to respect the puppy and his playthings. Adult vigilance, whenever children and puppies are together, will help prevent accidents and injuries.

With Other Animals

Because the Bernese Mountain Dog breed was developed as a farmer's dog, it's critical that Berners also be socialized around other animals. Lucky Berners will live on a working farm and be exposed to multiple different species from puppyhood. Berners in more suburban settings can also learn to get along with other animals.

If a neighbor has a dog-friendly cat, introduce the two so that your Berner understands that interspecies friendships are possible. Don't allow your pup to chase a cat. If the pup is shy or fearful around cats or other dogs, make introductions slowly and carefully. Start from a distance. Let the puppy's natural curiosity take over. Keep him on a leash so that you have control over any circumstance. When the puppy displays good attention to you with the distraction of another animal, reward him with praise. Always end these sessions on a positive note, whether you give him a good hug and rubdown, reward with something very tasty like chicken or liver, or toss his favorite toy, like a Nylabone.

If your Berner's future involves herding competitions or work, take him to watch dog-on-stock interactions. Let him sit on the opposite side of a fence from ducks, sheep, and cattle. Again, go slowly to make the experience a positive association for your young Berner, and leave while he still wants to investigate. He will be eager the next time you take him down to a farm to sit and watch the other animals, and he'll form a positive life view.

Training Your Bernese Mountain Dog   77

With New Places

Begin to expand your Berner's world by taking him on walks off your own property (once he's received the required vaccinations). He's ready for big-puppy training classes, where he will meet and greet other dogs, larger and smaller. Drive him around town and introduce him to tellers at the bank drive-in window, the order takers at the fast food restaurant, or the car wash attendant. Watch for delivery of your mail, and take your puppy out to meet the postal worker. Ask your friends to visit, treats in hand, to play in your house with your Berner puppy.

Introduce your Berner to as many different people as you can.

Ask strangers to stop and pet your Berner to further his education. Introduce him to as many different places, people, and pets as you can.

A good rule to follow is to take your puppy to two new places each week, introduce him to two new people, and add two new stimuli, like the sound of a motorcycle or barking dogs at a dog show. If your puppy seems overwhelmed by the new people, places, and things, cut back to one new location, sound, or person. Generally, the more you teach a Berner puppy on a regular basis, the better adjusted he will be as a grown dog.

Warning Signs

During any socialization excursion, watch your Berner for signs of discomfort in his new situation. If he tucks his tail between his legs, tries to hide behind you, drops his ears or pulls them back against his skull, then take a few steps back. Feed him treats or pieces of high-quality kibble during introductions to new people, places, or other animals. If he seems willing to investigate, allow that behavior. Always intervene to stop play between your dog and other animals or children if your Berner puppy hesitates.

You, the owner, must be vigilant and protective of your puppy, making sure that accidents and emotional traumas are prevented.

Crate Training

Positive training includes introduction to a crate, a place where your growing Bernese Mountain Dog will sleep, eat, and learn how to keep himself amused during hectic family times. A crate becomes a dog's personal refuge, a place he can retreat to if he is overwhelmed by other dogs in the household, children, deliveries, or loud noises. The crate is also the easiest, most important tool in the Berner's housetraining journey. Additionally, a dog who travels in a crate in a vehicle is less likely to be stressed during trips to and from the vet, and a dog who is acclimated to a crate won't resist it during times of convalescence from illness or surgery.

Crates are made of hard plastic, heavy wire, or furniture-grade wood. The best crates have adequate ventilation and no sharp edges that could injure a dog. A growing Bernese Mountain Dog can be put in the largest crates available, as many manufacturers now include dividers that can be moved. As the puppy grows, the space increases.

Some puppies appreciate a crate pad, while other Berner puppies shred anything in the crate. You'll know within a day if you have a lounger or a shredder.

How to Crate Train

Because Bernese Mountain Dogs appreciate being as close to their humans as possible, crate location is important. Some owners put the dog's crate in the kitchen or corner of the family room. With young puppies, it's helpful to also have a second crate in the bedroom so that when the puppy cries at night to go potty, you will hear him and respond. Wherever his crate is located, teach young children and overenthusiastic adults that if the puppy crawls into his crate, he must be left alone. This will teach the pup that his crate is his safe refuge.

Feed your Berner pup in his crate so that he forms positive associations with the enclosure. Between mealtimes, teach him that his crate is fun. Toss pieces of kibble or tasty treats into the back of the crate, leave the crate door open, and encourage him to go find the food. Let him repeat this game of "go find" several times a day.

When he willingly enters his crate for praise and a treat, close the door briefly. Extend the time that your Berner pup is inside his crate; it might take a day or two before he is comfortable and quiet in his crate with the door closed, but if he is acclimated slowly and has something to occupy his brain, then he will accept his crate as a friendly place. Puppy-appropriate toys, especially Nylabones or other toys that are stuffed with kibble, cheese, peanut butter, or other treats, can

Housetraining is the process of teaching your Berner where and when he can pee and poop.

your Berner where and when he can pee and poop, goes smoothly if a crate is utilized. A puppy doesn't want to sleep in a dirty enclosure, so a crate will help him learn to control his bladder and bowels. You can help your puppy learn appropriate potty skills if you develop a schedule and stick to the same routine. Don't leave the housetraining duties to children or to other adults who just don't want the responsibility.

How to Housetrain

A puppy will need to eliminate first thing in the morning, after meals, after every nap, and after hard play sessions. When he starts to sniff the floor, begins to squat, or turns in circles, he probably needs to eliminate.

Spend a few minutes enticing your puppy to enter and exit his crate, either to retrieve a toy or find bits of cheese. Then take him outside to a designated potty place. Because he has just expended energy in play, he is likely to squat and eliminate. When he does, throw a party! Tell him how wonderful he is, and pair words with his action that you want him to associate. "Good pee," "Good poop," and "Good potty," said in an upbeat, happy voice, will help him understand that you are pleased with his behavior. Take another few minutes to play, but do not allow him to explore the area or to play until he has finished his potty duties.

be put in the crate.

Never use the crate for punishment. With a breed as needy for human companionship as the Bernese Mountain Dog, it should be used only when a young pup cannot be supervised, during housetraining, and as a place for him to sleep, secure from other dogs or children. Depending on his age and your family's needs, don't crate a Berner for longer than his bladder can wait. This can be an hour up to about four hours.

Housetraining

Housetraining, the process of teaching

Once he has eliminated, explored, played, dug in the dirt, or other appropriate puppy play, and worn himself out, put him back in his crate and shut the door. He may pout, whine, or even shriek, but ignore his little tantrums. He'll probably sleep for another couple of hours. When he wakes and begins to fuss, immediately pick him up and carry him outside. Don't wait to put on his leash to walk him outside because you want to avoid an "almost made it" moment. Place him on the ground on his potty spot. As soon as he is successful, heap praise on him.

Stick to the schedule: Potty times are after every meal, after every nap, and right before the family retires at night. A schedule will help your Berner pup learn some self-control. He'll learn that if he whines, you will attend to his needs. If you take him outside and he does not potty, then put him back in his crate for five minutes. Take him outside again, and when he potties, praise him!

Housetraining Accidents

Housetraining should progress over the first couple of weeks. You'll learn to recognize your Berner's whines when he needs to go out versus the whines of "I'm bored and you need to fix this situation." Housetraining is a partnership, where success or failure rests squarely on your shoulders. If your pup seems unable to control his bladder or bowels inside his

Carpets, rugs, and floors can retain the scent of urine and feces, and dogs will use that area again unless the scent is eliminated.

crate after a month, have his veterinarian check him for infection, parasites, or a structural condition.

Also, many puppies regress in their housetraining at about four or five months of age. They are just busy thinking about other things, or the responsible adult has become complacent with the schedule. Regroup and start again.

Clean any accidents thoroughly with either a commercial or homemade product that will get rid of the lingering odor. Carpets, rugs, and floors can retain the scent of urine and feces, attracting puppies to use that area again unless the scent is eliminated. Usually the carpets, underlying pads, and rugs will need to be soaked with a cleaning solution, then dabbed with a dry cloth until the odor is gone.

Basic Commands

Training basic commands also commences on the day your Bernese Mountain Dog joins the family. Use positive training techniques with a clicker, treats, and a calm tone of voice while teaching him the basics. His obedience lessons will help him to become a dog who will be welcomed by extended family, friends, and neighbors.

Sit

The *sit* is one of the easiest skills to teach. A puppy who sits on command is easier to manage and will help you manage his behavior until he learns more self control. For example, when you teach your Berner to sit when the doorbell rings, he is less likely to jump up on visitors when the door opens.

How to Teach *Sit*

To teach the *sit*:

1. Get on your puppy's level, either on the floor or in a chair next to him.
2. Hold a treat close to his nose and let his head follow the treat as you move your hand up.
3. As his head moves up, his butt will lower.
4. When his butt hits the floor, release the treat to his mouth. Immediately praise him for his brilliance.

FINDING A TRAINER

Ask your breeder, veterinarian, local kennel clubs, and friends whose dogs are well behaved for trainer recommendations. Visit classes without your dog. Ask questions of other students. Berners, especially, respond to trainers who use positive rather than aversive methods.

Every time your Berner's rump hits the floor, tell him "Good *sit!*"

5. Repeat multiple times every day. Pair the behavior with the word "sit."

Don't hold the treat so high that your Berner tries to jump up for it. Instead, hold it in your closed hand just high enough that he stretches his neck. Every time his rump hits the floor, tell him "Good *sit!*" This is a great game for children in the house to play with your Berner.

Repetitions are important, but the Bernese Mountain Dog will tire of multiple reps. Rather, play the *sit* game with your Berner in short bursts multiple times every day. Reinforce the *sit* in other situations, like mealtimes. Have him sit before you put his food bowl on the floor or before

you open the door to take him on a walk. If he breaks the *sit*, remind him of his job with a quiet "Oops, try again" before you open the door. If this command is reinforced every time you ask your Berner to sit away from the door, he will be less likely to bolt and run when the door opens. In this respect, the *sit* command can be a lifesaver.

Come

The *come* command is another useful tool that can be used to manage annoying puppy behaviors until your dog is older and wiser. This command helps keep a dog out of trouble or gives him a job to do. If your Berner escapes the fenced yard or bolts out an open door, the command can also save his life. This foundation skill is one that you and your Bernese Mountain Dog will use and refine for the rest of his life.

How to Teach *Come*

To teach the *come*:

1. Clip a light line to your dog's collar and let him drag it around.
2. After he is accustomed to the line, pick up the end and hold it as you follow him around the yard. As he gets used to this, he'll begin to understand that the two of you are attached.
3. With your clicker (or voice marker word "yes") and a few treats, walk backward, encouraging him to follow along. When he twirls around and comes toward you, click and treat. Tell him that he's the cleverest dog in the world.
4. Begin to pair the behavior with the word "come." Every time he responds correctly, praise and reward him. Make the *come* command a game that your puppy wants to play.

Don't get in the bad habit of yelling "Come come come come" multiple times if your dog does not respond. Remember the one-word, one-command rule: Once your dog understands the command, if he does not come on the first command, go to him and gently guide him to where you want him to be. If you stand in the yard or at the door and holler repeatedly, he either doesn't understand the command yet or you are expecting too much too soon.

Never call a dog to come for discipline. If so, you will teach him to associate the command with a negative consequence. If your dog is behaving badly, always go to him rather than calling him to you.

Stay

The *stay* command is one of the hardest for puppies and young dogs to master. Asking a Berner, who only wants to sit

The goal with *stay* is to teach your dog that his job is to remain right where he is until given further instructions.

on his owner's feet or lean against her while she is in the kitchen, to stay put in another area, is almost asking too much! Like the other basic commands, however, the *stay* is a lifesaver. A dog who is taught to stay won't chase a duck in a pen or charge a cow in a field. The Berner who understands *stay* can also go on to more advanced obedience or rally competitions.

The goal with *stay* is to teach your dog that his job is to remain right where he is until given further instructions.

How to Teach *Stay*
To teach the *stay*:
1. Put a leash on your dog and have him sit comfortably next to you.
2. Wave a flat palm toward his muzzle and say "Stay."
3. Step in front of your dog, wait a few seconds, and then step back beside him.
4. Reward him for not breaking his *stay*.
5. If he moves, calmly say "Oops," or "Uh uh" and put him back where he was initially. Again, give the *stay* command along with the hand signal
6. Practice this multiple times every day in different locations.
7. After rewarding him with praise and a treat for success, teach him a release word, or the word you will say when it's time for him to be released from the *stay*. A good release word is "okay."

Down
The *down* command is a good management tool that helps keep the Berner out of trouble and out from underfoot. This behavior is one of the most difficult for many dogs to master because it's a submissive posture. A shy or fearful Bernese Mountain Dog might have more trouble learning or performing a *down*, so go slowly while teaching this skill. Use a happy voice, lots of praise, and good treats while training.

How to Teach *Down*
To teach the *down*:
1. Hold a very tasty treat in your closed hand and place it at your dog's muzzle.
2. When he notices the scent of the treat, move your hand toward the floor. A young dog or puppy should follow the hand that hides the treat.
3. While the dog's head follows your hand, move your hand along the floor in front of him. His body will follow his head, and once he stretches out into a *down*, open your hand to let him eat the treat.
4. Repeat multiple times daily, and pair the behavior with the word "down."

If your Berner lunges towards your hand, say "Nope" and take your hand away before he can get to the treat. If he tries to sit up, break away and start again. Don't push him into a *down*.

The *down* command is a good management tool that helps keep the Berner out of trouble and out from underfoot.

Clever dog that he is, your Berner will try everything to get to the treat. He's showing effort and should not be punished for thinking. Encourage every little bit of progress until he understands the command. After a successful attempt, always release your dog from the *down* and run off to play with him.

Walk Nicely on Leash

The ability to walk a large dog like a Bernese Mountain Dog on a loose leash is not just easier on his owner's arms and shoulders. A dog who doesn't lunge or pull at the end of his lead also shows your neighbors and friends that you have trained him to be a good member of the community. Additionally, a Berner who walks attentively next to his owner is less likely to become fearful in new situations.

Your dog has already begun to learn the *come* command on leash and to understand that the leash connects the two of you. It's time to begin to train him to walk politely and calmly by your side.

How to Teach *Walk Nicely on Leash*

To teach loose-leash walking:

1. Attach his leash to his buckle collar and say "Let's go" using your happy voice. Put treats in your left side pocket or a bait bag.
2. Encourage his forward motion by patting your left leg. When he is close to your side, pop a treat in his mouth.

TRAINING POINTERS

✓ Berners need positive training methods.
✓ Socialize a Berner with variety.
✓ Crates help with housetraining.
✓ Train your Berner every day.
✓ Teach him to sit for his dinner or before going out the door for a walk.
✓ Train the *come* as a game.
✓ Practice the *stay* multiple times and in various locations every day.
✓ Practice the *down* during quiet time.
✓ Teach loose-leash walking a few steps at a time.

3. Every few steps stop to praise him for being in the correct place.
4. When he forges ahead or lags behind, stop to let him wander to the end of his leash.
5. The slight leash tension will cause him to turn around. As soon as you feel the slack in the line, click or say your verbal praise marker. Praise and treat when he bounces back to you.
6. When he pulls, practice the "be a tree" principle, stopping all motion. His unwanted behavior will self-correct. Wait him out if he doesn't come back to your side.

Loose-leash walking takes a dedicated owner who allows her dog to make mistakes and has the patience to teach him the proper behavior. You want your Berner to believe that you are the most exciting person or thing he will ever encounter during his daily strolls. Given the Berner's temperament, he's probably already attached to your side, but he still will encounter distractions. Other people and their dogs, postal workers, garbage collectors, cats, squirrels, and cyclists might be common distractions for your dog. You don't want him to hide behind you or to investigate every interesting scent or sight along your walk.

If he's too excited to exhibit self-control, then have him sit until the distraction passes. Turn your walks into a game by running in the opposite direction, and he will run with you to find the party. When he catches up to you, stop to reward him with a cookie.

Practice and consistency are important. Once your Bernese Mountain Dog can walk on a loose leash, begin to pair the behavior with the *heel* command. This means "stay close to my left leg whether we are stopped or walking." Take a few steps with your dog in *heel* position, treat, and praise. Practice, practice, and more practice are required to teach your dog the *heel* position.

Chapter
7

Solving Problems
With Your
Bernese Mountain Dog

Despite their reputation as easygoing, gentle dogs, Bernese Mountain Dogs can present with problem behaviors. Recently the most disturbing trend is a tendency toward shyness, but proper socialization can help mitigate the behavior. Puppies who are products of puppy mills or backyard breeders have more problems with shyness or fearfulness—and problem behaviors in general—because their emotional development hasn't been nurtured. Problems that seem minor during puppyhood are only magnified in adult dogs, however. In an older dog, these issues can be helped with the proper training.

Dogs who develop problems are dogs who are bored, dogs who don't receive enough human interaction, or dogs who are not properly trained from the beginning. Also, dogs will repeat behaviors that they find intrinsically rewarding. Some behaviors are expected in dogs, like digging and chewing. Others are appropriate for this particular breed, like barking to announce the approach of other people. But most behaviors that owners describe as problems or as destructive actions are normal for dogs.

One of the most disturbing trends recently with Berners is a tendency toward shyness, but proper socialization can help mitigate the behavior.

TYPICAL BERNESE PROBLEM BEHAVIORS

Q: Which problem behaviors are typical for the breed and easily managed?

A: "The breed's problem behaviors are the same as most dogs: barking, chewing inappropriately, digging, and jumping on people. Addressing these behaviors at an early age can make a big difference. These dogs will be big by most people's standards and should be trained early. Socialization from eight weeks on will help prevent behaviors such as nipping, aggression, and being shy or fearful. Those behaviors can be very bad in an older dog and harder to address but can be improved upon with the proper training."

—Jim Durrance, owner/handler/trainer and draft judge for the Bernese Mountain Dog Club of America (BMDCA)

Some can be avoided, others can be mitigated, and some problems can be prevented.

When a Bernese Mountain Dog develops inappropriate behaviors, the consequences can be worse than those of smaller dogs. A Berner who digs in the yard, obviously, digs deeper. A Berner who decides to chew the furniture will do greater damage in the house. A Berner who jumps up can hurt the people around him, just because of his size.

Proper management can help Berner owners solve their dog's issues. Proper socialization helps some dogs, but serious issues must be handled by a highly trained professional who understands canine behavior. Never try to "fix" a serious behavior issue, such as aggression, according to popular Internet or television training advice. You will need an in-home canine behaviorist consultation before beginning a behavior modification program. The Bernese Mountain Dog Club of America (BMDCA) (www.bmdca.org) has a comprehensive network of breeders, owners, handlers, and trainers who make themselves available to Berner owners. Even if you are not a member of this parent club, members will happily try to help any Berner owner solve problem behaviors. Because too many Bernese Mountain Dogs end up in rescue groups because owners cannot or will not train their big dogs, the club works hard to prevent re-homing.

Aggression

Aggression is a serious problem that should never be ignored. This extreme temperament issue is cited as one of the main reasons for surrender to an animal shelter. Sometimes, however, an owner might mistake normal canine communication as aggression. Aggression is considered a range of behaviors that can manifest as snarling, growling, snapping, biting, and attacking. Because aggression can escalate without warning, the victim might be another dog in the home, a child, or an adult.

How to Manage It

Because aggression is so complex and challenging and the consequences can be disastrous, the need for a canine behaviorist is absolute. Do not try to fix an aggression issue without professional help from a canine behavior specialist. (See section "Seeking Professional Help.")

An aggressive dog should never be left unsupervised, must be confined to a crate or other enclosed quarters, nor can he be allowed typical family interaction. Solving an aggression problem is very difficult, requiring a level of commitment from one principal caretaker who is willing to work with her dog.

Behaviorists, veterinarians, and dog trainers with experience with the problem should be consulted. They each can offer help within their fields of expertise, whether it's training advice, behavior modification techniques, or medications.

Usually, dogs who display aggressive tendencies will not be accepted in a rescue group for retraining and re-homing. The resources and time required to solve this problem is beyond the financial, physical, and emotional abilities of many rescuers or shelter staff.

Barking

Because the Bernese Mountain Dog was originally bred as a farmer's companion and watchdog, barking to announce a stranger's approach is an expected and

For most Berners, barking to announce a stranger's approach is an expected and common breed trait.

MEDICAL/PHYSICAL CAUSES OF PROBLEM BEHAVIORS

When faced with a problem behavior, especially one that presents suddenly, always look for a medical or physical cause. Don't just assume that the dog has turned into a "bad dog." A Bernese Mountain Dog who begins to growl when his owner strokes his back might be in pain, for example. Get a thorough vet check before jumping to any conclusions.

common breed trait. Most Berners, once they see their owner's acceptance of a visitor, will cease any vocalizations. Others, however, continue to bark.

Dogs bark for different reasons, and some owners are challenged to find out why their Berner engages in excessive barking. For most dogs, regardless of the breed, barking is a sign of boredom. He could be frustrated or may feel isolated. Because Berners are incredibly devoted to their owners and extremely needy, a Berner who barks too much could be seeking more attention or affection. A barking Berner could be saying "Hey, play with ME! NOW!", or he could be asking for more work.

Before deciding that your Bernese Mountain Dog is barking inappropriately, take a careful inventory of the time you actually spend with your dog. An honest evaluation of your interaction, followed by more time spent together, could solve your dog's excessive barking.

How to Manage It

If your dog's barking is truly a nuisance, this is one of the easiest problems to manage. At the same time that you increase his playtime or activities, teach him when his barking is inappropriate. If you find that he barks at certain stimuli, such as a child bicycling past your house, you can desensitize him to that visual stimulus. Start by teaching the *quiet* command. If your dog barks at a neighbor walking past the house, for example, allow one or two barks and then say "Quiet." Interrupt his barking by using a shaker can, which could be an empty soda can or water bottle with a few coins inside it. Startle your dog with a shaker, and as soon as he is quiet, tell him "Good quiet" and offer a treat. The noise from the shaker should not be used as a punishment. Instead, it's a method to redirect your Berner's attention away from the neighbor. You can also try to ignore him when he barks, then reward him when he stops. This will take huge

Some dogs bark out of fear of noises like thunderstorms or holiday fireworks.

behaves. Eventually, you want your dog to sit quietly while he is introduced to your visitors, at which time he will get his special treat, plus some ear rubs for his reward.

Some dogs bark out of fear of noises, like holiday fireworks or thunderstorms. In those cases, make sure your Berner doesn't have an underlying medical condition such as an ear infection. If he is medically sound, you can either try to desensitize him to the noise or shield him from the stimulus. Background music can redirect your dog's auditory system. If he is truly thunderphobic, your veterinarian can prescribe anti-anxiety medication. Don't coddle a phobic dog. Instead, in an upbeat voice, say "Oh, you silly boy! Let's just sit and watch the storm." Some storm-phobic dogs have very high levels of cortisol, a stress hormone, present in their bloodstream. Those dogs do well with medication management. Others might just need calming herbs or holistic remedies. Check with your breeder, trainer, or vet for names of specific natural remedies that could help your dog.

amounts of patience on your part.

If your Berner barks at approaching visitors, remember that this is inherent in his breed personality. If he won't quiet down after you welcome your visitor and make proper introductions, this is a problem. With help from a friend, give your dog a special high-value treat if he is quiet once your friend has been welcomed at the door. Advance this over several days, as the friend is on the threshold and then inside the front door. At the same time, teach your dog to sit when someone enters and give him praise and a special treat when he

If your Berner is barking because he's bored, try some different activities with him. Join a group of other dog owners to teach him how to pull a cart, or to track.

Chewing

Dogs chew. This is a natural behavior, as a dog puts his mouth on things in his environment to help him figure out his world. If your Bernese Mountain Dog puppy is teething, he might chew the arms off your wingchair. If your adult Berner is chewing inappropriately, he's probably bored.

Intervention is successful when the owner is committed to retraining her dog. She must be willing to teach her dog what is and what is not an acceptable chew toy.

How to Manage It

To manage chewing, keep personal belongings and valuables out of sight and reach. If your Berner has chosen your sofa pillows as his new favorite chew toys, either remove the pillows or use baby gates to keep him from that room, unless you can supervise him.

Don't allow your Berner to chew on an old shoe, expecting him to differentiate between your new heels and his old shoe.

Don't allow your Berner to chew on an old shoe, expecting him to differentiate between your new heels and his old shoe. Be realistic in your expectations. Sometimes a dog is just being a dog when he chews up your remote control or eyeglasses. If you catch him in the act, interrupt him by offering a more acceptable item, like a raw marrow bone. And if you haven't caught him in the act but come home to find the house strewn with the stuffing from his dog bed, never scold him. He won't know why he's suddenly in trouble.

Mitigate your Berner's destructive chewing by giving him opportunities for mental and physical stimulation. Give him interactive toys that dispense kibble, or give him a toy meant for strong, aggressive chewers.

Additionally, spray furniture with bitter-tasting substances. These products are pet safe and can be used frequently and liberally. If your Berner is fond of the deck posts, cover them with heavy aluminum or chicken wire to deter his chewing. Usually, creative management techniques will outwit young dogs until they grow up, mature, and don't feel the need to chew on your house.

Digging

This is another normal canine behavior, although dogs dig for several reasons. Some are trying to escape a threat, or

PUPPY SOCIALIZATION

According to breeder/owner/handler and rescue coordinator Amy Kessler, Bernese Mountain Dog puppies who have not been properly socialized will develop temperament issues that lead to problem behaviors. "All puppies, all breeds, go through a fear period, but with Berners, that is more apparent because they have such soft temperaments," she says. "This usually happens sometime between five and eight weeks. This is when a bowl they have been eating out of every day all of a sudden becomes scary, or a toy they have played with all along becomes scary.

"It is just a part of their developing a personality and temperament, and anything that happens during this time sets their temperament for life. This is why we see so many temperament problems in dogs who come from [puppy] mills or backyard breeders who don't know the breed."

they dig because they are after prey. Dogs dig for entertainment or to get attention because they know from learned experience that digging in the garden will attract their humans, who will come running from the house. Digging becomes self-rewarding, too. Bernese Mountain Dogs who dig are engaging in grand fun.

How to Manage It

Rather than eliminating this behavior, it's best to just try to manage your digging dog. If you don't want him to dig holes in a specific area of the yard, restrict his access. Roll wire fencing over that area, burying any sharp edges to prevent injury.

If you are outside with your dog and can supervise his activity, you can keep him on a leash or long line. Never put a line on a dog when you are not with him because he could accidently snare the line injuring himself, or worse.

If he starts to dig while you are with him, use the shaker can as a distraction. Then, offer your dog something more interesting to do.

Consider giving your Berner an area of the yard where he's allowed to pursue his passion. Some owners bury treasures like old bones or weather-safe toys in loose sand or soil.

House Soiling

Any Bernese Mountain Dog who suddenly begins to soil his bedding, his crate, or the house needs to be evaluated by a veterinarian for illness or injury. Common illnesses that can cause a dog to soil the house include urinary tract infections or parasitic gastrointestinal infections or infestations. Some dogs manifest pain by losing control of their bladders or bowels.

How to Manage It

A young Bernese Mountain Dog who soils the house has probably been allowed too much freedom too soon, without supervision. As a pup gets older, when he is taken outside he will be distracted by interesting details of his environment. Then he may forget the purpose of the potty area. When this happens, don't let your dog take all day to relieve himself. When you give him his usual amount of potty time, if he doesn't take advantage of it, put him back in his crate for 10 to 20 minutes. He will understand very soon why he has been confined. Take him back outside, and praise him for a successful outing.

An owner who doesn't notice that her puppy or young dog hasn't eliminated might rush her dog or just assume that he's taken care of his potty detail. She might stand at the door while he goes outside, and when he comes back in she rewards him with a treat. Then, he promptly squats on the kitchen floor. When this happens, never blame your dog, and never rub his nose in the mess or swat him with a newspaper. Rather, hit yourself in the head and repeat "I will pay better attention to my dog."

Each accident that happens is almost always a failure on the part of the owner. Some young dogs are expected to go unattended for too long, or the owner just hasn't noticed her dog whimpering by the door. If your Berner has an indoor accident, try to interrupt him in the act. If he is still small enough, scoop him up and carry him outside to his potty area. If you are too late, ask your dog to forgive your lapse, calmly clean up the mess, and vow not to give him so much freedom.

As a pup gets older, when he is taken outside he may be distracted by interesting details of his environment and forget the purpose of the potty area.

Adolescent dogs between four and five months of age can backslide in their housetraining. This is usually because their brains are thinking about things other than their full bladder.

Jumping Up

Canine language is complicated. Dogs sniff, lick, and body slam each other. They roll each other on the ground, play-bow, and jump up in each other's faces. These are perfectly acceptable forms of dog communication. But when a dog uses his normal methods of greeting in an unacceptable way toward people, he gets in trouble. When he's so overjoyed to see you, whether you've been gone all day or just gone to get the newspaper from the driveway, he might jump up and give your face a swipe with his huge tongue.

With a dog as large and heavy as a full-grown Bernese Mountain Dog, jumping up on people can be dangerous. This attention-seeking behavior can injure children and adults. You must teach your dog to keep "four on the floor" at all times.

How to Manage It

The *sit* and *stay* obedience lessons are critical to teach a dog that he cannot jump up on people. If the dog is taught that more gentle greetings are rewarded with praise or a treat, and if the owner is consistent, this behavior can be trained. All family members must be strict about the rules: no praise, no petting, and no treats unless the dog sits quietly during greetings.

When your Berner jumps up, turn your back and say "Off." As soon as all four of his paws are on the ground, quietly praise him. Don't be overly enthusiastic in your praise, lest he get too excited. Then give him the *sit* command. Again, praise him quietly and offer a small treat. Keep your voice command soft, and only treat him when he responds to the *off* and then the *sit*.

Keep a secure container of treats by all entry doors. Every time someone comes into the house, whether a family member or visitor, ask her to bring a treat in for your dog. When he sits quietly, he can have the treat.

Also, if there is a time of day that is more hectic, such as when children return from after-school activities or adults come home from work, try to put your dog in a *down-stay* before the family streams into the house.

To teach the *down-stay*:

1. Lure the dog into a *down*, then treat and/or praise him.
2. Say "Stay," wave your hand in front of his muzzle, step in front of him, and reward him before returning to his side.
3. Give the *stay* command, take a few steps away, return, and treat.
4. Build the distance and duration over several weeks.

Every time he behaves, he should get a treat, a gentle hug, or quiet praise.

Don't ignore the dog who doesn't jump, either. Every time your Berner responds to his commands and refrains from jumping, reward him. If he isn't praised, he'll begin the attention-seeking jumping behavior all over again.

When your Berner is taken out and about, he must never be allowed to jump on strangers or friends. If he is too excited and cannot contain his enthusiasm, remove him from the situation. Don't put a young Berner in a position that he is not ready to handle emotionally or that he is not trained for properly because you'll be setting him up for failure.

Nipping

Berners should be taught from puppyhood that they cannot put their teeth on human skin. Ever. Nipping behaviors between littermates or a dam and her puppies are common and the main way that young puppies are taught how to behave with each other. Some pups, however, naturally want to mouth human hands that reach down to pet them or feed them. This is not usually an aggression issue but rather a communication error.

A Bernese Mountain Dog should be confident, alert, good natured, and gentle with children, other animals, and adults.

How to Manage It

A Bernese Mountain Dog who nips needs to be taught that if his teeth touch skin, he will lose all his privileges. He gets no attention, which he desperately wants and needs.

If your Berner nips when you reach to pet him, redirect his attention with an appropriate chew toy, such as a Nylabone. Offer the toy with one hand while petting him with your other hand. Pet him for short periods of time because the longer your hand is on your Berner, the more excited he will get and the more likely that he will nip. Also, rather than pet the top of his head, pet his sides, chest, or under his chin, which he may view as less threatening.

If your Berner nips you, holler in a very loud voice "Ouch!" and then ignore him. Turn away, leave the room, or step away from his vicinity. He might be overexcited, needing a brief time-out in his crate.

Repetitions of your voice corrections, along with confinement of the dog, can help him understand that his action caused the adverse reaction. Because a Bernese Mountain Dog craves his person, he will not want to continue his bad behavior.

When he is successful, no longer grabbing for the hand that reaches to pet him, give him the praise that he deserves, along with your undivided, loving attention.

Seeking Professional Help

A Bernese Mountain Dog should be confident, alert, good natured, and gentle with children, other animals, and adults. These dogs should never be shy, although this trait is a disturbing trend among dogs who come from backyard breeders and puppy mills. While a dog's underlying temperament can be inherited, it can also be influenced along the way by good or bad experiences. Also, dogs can develop problem behaviors at any age. Just because an adult dog has navigated the normal, destructive puppy age does not guarantee that he will settle into a calm, mature dog who can behave properly all the time.

If a negative behavior presents suddenly, then a veterinary consult is always required. Pain, injury, illness, parasites, and a host of other canine afflictions can bring about a change in a dog's behavior.

Any dog with a problem behavior not easily resolved through appropriate training or management should be assessed by a canine behaviorist. Various professionals offer evaluation and training advice. Some are trainers

Any dog with a problem behavior not easily resolved through appropriate training or management should be assessed by a canine behaviorist.

PROBLEM BEHAVIOR CHECKLIST

✓ Train your dog to prevent some problem behaviors.
✓ Bernese Mountain Dogs should bark to warn the owner of visitors. Bored dogs bark excessively. Train a *quiet* command or use a shaker can to interrupt barking.
✓ Supervise your Berner to prevent chewing, and give him age-appropriate chew toys.
✓ Exercise your dog to prevent digging, give him a place where he's allowed to dig, or bury "treasure" for him to dig up and enjoy.
✓ Get veterinary attention for sudden house soiling. Properly crate train to prevent accidents, and hit yourself in the head with a newspaper if your dog has an accident because it's your fault!
✓ Teach the *sit* to prevent jumping up and reward your dog for "four on the floor."
✓ Yell "Ouch" if your dog nips, then pet his back, sides, or chest rather than his face or head, which he may see as threatening. Also, give a toy with one hand while your other hand pets the dog.

with many years of experience. Some might have credentials from professional affiliations but might not have experience treating your dog's particular issue. Still other professionals are veterinarians who specialize or sub-specialize in behavior, employing a combination of medications or behavior modifications to help their patients. Before writing a check, ask any professional if she has direct experience treating your dog's problem. Get references from breeders, trainers, and other dog owners to find a person who can help.

Canine behavior specialist Dorothy Dunning, IACP (International Association of Canine Professionals), says that owners who are exasperated by their dog's problems need an attitude adjustment. Generalized, deliberate aggression or extreme fearfulness is a serious cause for concern. "Most owners do not recognize real aggression or serious fear, but a professional should be able to do that and suggest the best treatment. When the owner–trainer learns to communicate with the dog consistently and often, in a way the dog can understand, the behavior usually improves markedly."

Dunning adds that owners typically know when they need professional help. "If you have tried the techniques described and found them wanting, or even if you don't really want to train the dog, consulting a professional is a reasonable next step," she says.

Activities With Your Bernese Mountain Dog

A breed as versatile as the Bernese Mountain Dog, who wants to please his owner, can excel at several canine sports. From herding to tracking, obedience to agility, a Berner who is properly trained and conditioned can do very well. Canine sports also enhance the owner–dog bond, which is so important to this breed. The Berner is also a willing traveler with his family.

Sports and Activities

Bernese Mountain Dogs make great participants in a variety of sports and activities. Whichever sport or activity you attempt, know that basic obedience training is necessary. An obedience-trained Berner will take more readily to a cart harness or to directions from a stock handler, for example. He will also become a more confident dog, which is important for a shy or timid Berner.

Agility

Agility is a fast-paced sport that includes jumps, weaves, and contact obstacles. Dogs are judged on time and willingness to follow their handler's commands on the agility course. Despite their size, Berners can compete in agility if certain precautions are taken. Before a Bernese Mountain Dog participates fully in this sport, he should be physically mature to protect his joints. The agility obstacles—

Bernese Mountain Dogs make great participants in a variety of sports and activities.

jumps, weave poles, A-frame, dog walk, tunnels and chutes, and teeter—should be taught slowly over many months.

Conformation (Dog Shows)

Bernese Mountain Dogs who closely adhere to the breed standard, can be exhibited in conformation shows. These "breed ring" dog shows are organized by several registries, notably the American Kennel Club (AKC) and the

Bernese Mountain Dogs who closely adhere to the breed standard can be exhibited in conformation shows.

United Kennel Club (UKC) in the United States. Dogs and bitches are judged based on how closely they resemble the ideal Bernese Mountain Dog as described by the breed standard. Conformation shows grew out of early gatherings, when breed enthusiasts would get together to compare dogs and select new breeding stock.

Conformation judges watch the dog's movement, along with structure. As they check his coat and dentition, they observe any temperament issues, such as shyness. Depending on how many Berners are entered at any one show, the best dog and the best bitch win points toward the Championship designation.

Puppies as young as three months

can be exhibited in breed "matches," which allow new handlers and dogs to gain experience in this sport. Also, children from 8 to 17 years old can compete in separate Junior Showmanship classes. Rather than judging the Berner, placements and awards are based on how the youngster handles her dog.

Specialty Bernese Mountain Dog shows are those where only that breed is exhibited. They are sponsored by regional clubs around the country. Additionally, the Bernese Mountain Dog Club of America (BMDCA) holds a National Specialty each year. The location rotates around the United States. Affiliated with the National Specialty are competitions in

DRAFT WORK

Q: When should a Bernese Mountain Dog start draft work?

A: "The following is what I have recommended over the years: Before any dog pulls any weight, he should be close to two years old, which allows the joints to mature. Also, even a mature dog needs to get in shape before pulling weight."

—Jim Durrance, owner/handler/trainer and draft judge for the Bernese
Mountain Dog Club of America (BMDCA)

tracking, drafting, rally, and obedience. A conformation win at a National Specialty is always reason for celebration and an honor for the dog, the owner, and the breeder.

Drafting and Herding

Two activities, herding and drafting, test a Berner's natural ability to do his historical job keeping a herd together or pulling a cart to market.

Drafting

Berners who are physically mature, about two years old, can participate in draft tests. This precaution reduces injury and protects the dog's joints, tendons, and muscles during critical growth periods.

The BMDCA holds draft tests that demonstrate a Berner's abilities to haul weight over a variety of terrains and distances, both with a handler and in more independent situations. The dog must work willingly and efficiently. Draft tests demonstrate control and responsiveness to the handler prior to, during, and after the dog is hitched to a cart or wagon. Obedience-like heeling patterns while the dog is hitched include turns, halts, and pace changes. Depending on the level, the dog is required to do group *stays* while hitched to loaded carts with the handler either in the ring or out of sight. Draft tests can be done with one dog or two Berners working side by side pulling the same cart.

A freight haul, which includes uphill and downhill slope changes, demonstrates the dog's ability to pull his laden cart with control and precision.

Carting is an activity that has usefulness around the home, too. A Berner who pulls a cart can help his owner around the garden or on a farm. He can participate in community parades or carry groceries home from the market.

A Berner should be introduced to the

harness in a safe and controlled manner. Let him sniff the leather or fabric, then put him in the harness and let him parade around in his new finery. When he is comfortable, he can begin to drag items hanging from the traces, such as empty jugs.

Introduce your Berner to his cart by letting him sniff it. Pull the cart alongside the dog while you walk him. Your Bernese Mountain Dog needs to be completely comfortable with the cart or wagon before he is hitched. Liberal use of praise and good treats, along with positive training methods, will make draft training a happy experience for your dog.

Regional BMDCA clubs offer classes and seminars to help novice owners get started in draft work. Mentors help to decide which type of harness will work best on an individual Berner. Carts and wagons can be borrowed, or some owners make their own based on the family's needs.

Titles earned through BMDCA draft tests are now accepted by the AKC and can be added to the dog's registered name as AKC titles.

Herding

The BMDCA also encourages Berner owners to explore herding with their dogs,

A Berner who pulls a cart can help his owner around the garden or on a farm or can participate in community parades or carry groceries home from the market.

DRAFTING PREP

Bernese Mountain Dog Club of America (BMDCA) draft judge Jim Durrance says that puppies as young as eight weeks should begin obedience training, learn their manners, and discover how to be friendly around other people. All of these basic skills are necessary for a good draft dog. When the Berner reaches six months of age, he can learn to wear a walking harness and pull an empty jug or cardboard box. During this time, the puppy can also be taught to turn left or right, go slow or fast, halt, and back up while he wears his draft harness. By 18 months of age, a cart can be attached to the dog's harness. Before adding weight to the cart, make sure that your young Berner becomes used to pulling an empty cart and can make turns slowly and safely. Add weight to the cart in 5-pound increments (2.5-kg), and pay attention to the terrain to keep your Berner safe while draft training.

a sport in which Berners herd ducks, sheep, or cows through chutes or into pens, depending on how the herding test is organized. The American Herding Breed Association (AHBA) allows Bernese Mountain Dogs to enter tests that show a dog's potential as a herding dog. In 2010, the AKC added Berners to the list of dog breeds eligible to earn AKC herding titles.

Herding with a Berner gives him an opportunity to use his inherent breed trait as a farmer's dog. This is a physically challenging activity and a great stimulation for a Berner's mind. A herding Berner won't be bored. Also, the teamwork between a handler and her Bernese Mountain Dog strengthens their deep bond.

Before taking your Berner to visit the local sheep farm, however, there are some important steps to take prior to entering a herding test or trial. Make sure that your Bernese Mountain Dog is physically fit before taking on the challenges of herding. Additionally, because this sport can be expensive, it may be out of reach for many Berner families. Training a dog to work different livestock often requires long-distance travel. Beginners should find an experienced trainer for private lessons. Some novice dogs might be nervous when first introduced to stock, and some fearful dogs might shy away from the sounds of a stock trial. A very experienced trainer who has had success with this breed on stock can help the Berner handler to understand her dog's reaction to stock and develop a training plan.

Even though a Bernese Mountain Dog continues to be a farm favorite in his native Switzerland, not every Berner will have the desire or the instinct necessary to be a successful herding dog. For those who do, however, the activity is rewarding for both dog and handler.

Obedience and Rally Obedience

An obedience-trained dog walks nicely in *heel* position, both on and off leash. He understands his owner's commands, whether verbal or signaled with hand motions. Obedience exercises range from a simple *stand* for a hands-on examination by the judge to group *sits* and *down-stays*. Because Berners were bred to work independently of their owners, they usually do well on more advanced obedience exercises that require them to work away from their handler.

Rally obedience, a competition that includes lower jump heights, is great for immature dogs and veterans who cannot jump the full heights of obedience. Like a car race, rally obedience has a starting point and a finish line. The course includes specific exercises, set up at specified stations, like right and left turns, pivots, *downs*, halts, and *stands*. The team could encounter any of the three obedience jumps: the bar, high, or broad jump. Novice dogs work on leash while more advanced teams work off

lead. Rally is a great introductory sport for a young Berner and for owners who have never participated in canine sports. The atmosphere is welcoming, and newcomers are celebrated and supported by long-time trainers.

Several organizations offer obedience and rally competitions. The AKC, UKC, the Association of Pet Dog Trainers (APDT), and the Australian Shepherd Club of America (ASCA) organize versions of rally or obedience trials open to Bernese Mountain Dogs. The rules vary by group, but most of the exercises are the same or very similar.

Find a nearby trial to take your family to watch the dogs and handlers. Ask

A Bernese who can easily adhere to basic obedience commands might be a good candidate for the sport.

some of the competitors where they take lessons, whether in rally or obedience. Most competitors welcome questions, and they all love to talk about their dogs. Get copies of the rules and regulations for each sport. Practice the required exercises with your dog. Whether you compete in obedience or rally, the journey with your Berner can lead to a more intense bond. And you will meet people who could become friends for life.

Keep in mind that orthopedic integrity is critical in a working Berner because obedience and rally require good jumping skills.

Therapy Work

A properly socialized and calm Bernese Mountain Dog excels at therapy dog work. He can comfort an ill or injured child or lay his head in the lap of a senior citizen.

His thick, silky coat is perfect for a patient in a rehabilitation hospital setting who can practice hand motions while brushing the dog. A cuddly, calm Berner can sit with a child in a library to listen while the young reader forms words, without passing judgment on a child's developing reading skills.

Because each Berner's personality is unique, while looking for a therapy dog group, try to find an organization that allows different settings. Your Berner might work best with Alzheimer's patients, or he might want to be with young adults who have developmental disabilities. The organization will help you decide which setting is best for your individual dog.

Therapy dogs must have solid basic obedience training. Some groups require that the dog have a Canine Good Citizen (CGC) certification from the AKC. The

Regardless of whether he wins or loses, participating in sports with your dog should be fun.

SPORTS AND SAFETY

Before starting any canine sports training or trialing, a Berner should be in good physical condition to prevent injury. His orthopedic integrity can be evaluated by a vet, which might include radiographs of a Berner's hips, knees, and elbows. His eyesight can also be checked to determine the presence of eye disease that could impair his ability to take jumps.

At the very least, your dog should lose any extra weight before embarking in agility, obedience, rally, tracking, herding, or drafting. Your veterinarian can help to assess his soundness and help develop a weight management program.

A Berner also needs to reach emotional maturity before he's asked to compete. Because this dog will do anything to please his owner, even if the task is beyond his physical abilities, he can hurt himself in the process. Rapidly growing youngsters are easily injured when paired with a novice handler or incompetent trainer.

With any sport or activity, good foundation obedience training is imperative. You should be able to call your dog off a jump in obedience; a solid *recall* and drop from a distance can help prevent injuries in stock work.

Learn proper warm-up and cool-down procedures for your canine partner. A program that includes stretching and massage techniques will help your Berner perform in peak condition. Find a canine rehabilitation specialist or chiropractor to help condition your dog. After a training session or a weekend of competition, watch your dog carefully for any sign of injury or overuse. Some dogs are excellent at masking discomfort, but others might favor a limb. Any time a dog refuses a jump or cannot put weight on a leg, a visit to the vet is warranted.

Make an honest assessment of your dog's physical and mental stamina before expecting him to compete safely in canine sports. If he's mature and healthy, a Bernese Mountain Dog can compete at the highest levels of all dog sports.

CGC proves a dog's ability to work around other dogs, respond to his owner's simple commands, and willingness to interact with strangers such as children. Other groups have more stringent requirements. The dog should be comfortable in all different situations. He should not spook around persons in wheelchairs or around those who use canes, walkers, or crutches. He should be calm around crowds and not excitable or anxious if a group of children suddenly rushes toward him.

Local, national, and international groups train, test, and certify therapy dogs. Most therapy dogs need more than the basic core vaccinations and must have veterinary health certificates. Human members of the team also go through training, making visits alongside longtime volunteers. Once both the dog and his owner have been trained and tested, the group will recommend placement in a facility as a volunteer team.

Tracking

Tracking is a canine sport that is less strenuous on a Bernese Mountain Dog's joints, but it's a sport that will challenge his mind and strengthen his body.

When traveling with your Berner, take plenty of extra water from home to minimize any stomach upset.

Tracking grew out of a dog's inborn ability to scent, search, and find. A Berner can excel at tracking once he understands the rules of scenting.

Although tracking is a vigorous outdoor activity, a Berner will do well if he is properly conditioned. Tests range from a basic Tracking Dog (TD) title, which ambles the dog over a few hundred yards (m), to the complex Variable Surface Track (VST). Some tracks are laid through open fields, while others have multiple direction changes through urban areas. The tracking dog follows the scent of the tracklayer over creeks and parking lots, around turns and through brush. Dogs are taught to alert the handler when the final article dropped by the tracklayer is found.

More information on tracking tests is available on the AKC's website; other organizations also put on eligibility tests.

Traveling With Your Berner

Because the Bernese Mountain Dog loves to be with his human family, it's reasonable to want to take him along on trips. Whatever the mode of travel and wherever you roam, keep in mind that a large dog will require more space, more travel supplies, higher costs, and take up more vacation time.

Don't forget to pack all the "stuff" that your Berner will need for his trip. Take plenty of extra water from your home to minimize any stomach upset that can occur when a dog drinks water from a different source. Pack or plan to purchase inexpensive bottled water along the way.

Measure out his food, whether it is kibble, canned, or raw. Each meal can be packaged in its own plastic or paper bag. Take the guesswork out of measuring on the road to make sure that your Berner eats what he needs—no more and no less.

Also, take an ample supply of disposal bags. At rest stops, restaurants, and hotels, follow local signs for the dog walk area.

Your dog's vaccination records should be stored in your vehicle or on a bag hung from the crate. Some states require that any person traveling through with a dog can be stopped for officers to check the animal's vaccination records. If traveling to an area where different organisms are prevalent, ask your vet if your Berner needs additional vaccinations. Make sure that your veterinarian's name and contact information are in your dog's paperwork as well as on a collar tag.

Car Travel

Car travel is the most popular method for Berner owners, but make sure that the dog has enough room in the automobile, van, or recreational vehicle. Because an unrestrained dog becomes a heavy missile during a car crash, a canine restraint system is the safest way to travel with a dog.

Because the Bernese Mountain Dog loves to be with his human family, it can be fun to travel with him.

A crate needs to be large enough for the Bernese Mountain Dog to stand up, turn around, and lie down. It should also be tied or strapped down to interior bolts or hooks to prevent it from shifting. A heavy wire crate works well for car travel. Window screens or reflective crate covers will help keep your Berner cool. Crate fans that run on batteries or right off your vehicle's power are also helpful.

If a crate isn't practical for your vehicle,

use a canine-specific harness or restraint system. The best car harnesses buckle directly into the car's seat belt, and the buckle is made of metal. Plastic buckles can break during a crash.

While driving, don't allow your dog to hang his head out an open window. This might look cute but can lead to unintended injuries. Dogs can get foreign objects embedded in their eyes, and on a road trip, you don't want to be sitting in an emergency veterinary clinic.

Although some dogs travel sans collar in their crate, for safety reasons, all dogs should wear collars and tags while in their crates. Some owners even attach short walking leashes to the dog's collar. In the event of an emergency, responders can safely handle a frightened dog who is already sporting a collar and leash.

Air Travel

Traveling with a Berner by air might work if you live close to a major airport or airline hub. Dogs must travel in a crate that meets shipping regulations. These are made of hard molded plastic or steel. Almost all dogs must travel as cargo, except for small dogs who fit at the owners feet inside the cabin. Major airlines now have restrictions on when dogs are allowed to fly. The time of day and especially the temperature are factors. Usually, airlines won't ship a dog in the cold of winter or the hottest days of summer. Airlines also have guidelines on

feeding and watering dogs pre- and post-flight.

Some major cities are serviced by a pet-only airline. The animals travel in their crates in the cabin rather than in a cargo hold. Check your airport to see if a pet-specific airline operates in your area.

Pet-Friendly Lodging

Hotels and motels have found new business by catering to pet owners. Many chains allowing dogs in guest rooms throw out the welcome mat for pets and their families. Before booking, though, call the specific hotel first to ask about the pet policy. Individual hotels or motels—regardless of the chain's policies—might not allow dogs. Some facilities allow only small- or medium-sized dogs. Pet fees are usually charged to offset any damage caused by a dog, and fees are higher for large dogs.

If you do take your Berner into a motel or hotel room, a few courtesies will help ensure that the facility will be available to the next family's dog. First, crate your dog every time he is alone in the room. Even if your Bernese Mountain Dog is the most mellow dog you've ever owned, and even if he's a seasoned traveler, things happen that cause dogs to react badly when owners are away. Thunderstorms, car alarms, hotel fire alarms, or loud noises from the next room can cause a dog to startle. A dog who is crated cannot cause damage to the room.

Check It Out

ACTIVITIES AND TRAVEL CHECKLIST

✓ Conformation shows reward dogs who meet the American Kennel Club (AKC) breed standard.

✓ Avoid full draft work until a Berner is two years old.

✓ A herding job tests a Berner's natural instincts on stock.

✓ Obedience training helps a Berner in any canine sport, and obedience trials test dog-and-handler teamwork.

✓ Rally puts less stress on a large dog's frame.

✓ Socialize a Berner thoroughly to prepare for therapy dog work.

✓ Tracking tests the Berner's scent abilities.

✓ Crate a Berner during travel, bring extra food and water, clean up his waste at hotels and rest stops, and pack his vaccination records.

Put a sheet of plastic under the crate in the room to protect the floor from unexpected accidents. Place an old sheet or blanket from home on top of the bedding, which will protect the hotel bed from all of your Berner's shedding hair. Never use a hotel bathroom to bathe your Berner because the pipes could clog, making you liable to pay for repairs.

Always follow the facility's guidelines about dog waste disposal. Some hotels and motels have generous large-dog exercise areas, but some have only a strip of grass. If you have taught your Bernese Mountain Dog to potty on command prior to any travel, you won't have to worry about his refusal to relieve himself unless he has a large green area. Also, ask if the lodging facility has a specific receptacle for dog waste. Nobody wants to exit a hotel room and get a whiff from a nearby trashcan full of dog waste.

Use common sense and common courtesy when you travel with your big dog so that the next travelers can enjoy pet-friendly lodging.

Health of Your
Bernese Mountain Dog

Many Berners enjoy good health well into old age, but the breed does have some significant health issues. A proactive owner who provides preventive care, watches vigilantly for illness or injury, and who understands the health challenges of the breed can help her dog enjoy a long and active life.

Choosing a Vet

The greatest advocate your Bernese Mountain Dog will ever have is you, his owner. Second to you, his best friend will be his veterinarian. This partnership will be very important to your dog because while he gives a lifetime of devotion to you, his vet will see him through some of his darkest days.

The breed's health issues are significant, some are hard to diagnose early, and others are very expensive to treat. But the right veterinarian will know something about the breed. She will know the signs of the serious illnesses that Berners are prone to develop and have access to cutting-edge Western medicines and techniques for diagnoses. She will also have an appreciation for ancient Eastern veterinary medicine such as acupuncture and Chinese herbs.

What to Look For

To find the right veterinarian for your Bernese Mountain Dog, ask your puppy's breeder if she has a favorite in your area. Neighbors and friends who are happy with their pets' health care are also valuable resources. There might be a university veterinary school in your area that can make recommendations, or a local or regional veterinary medical association. Groomers, trainers, and boarding facility operators will have networks of vets they like.

First impressions are important. Is the clinic clean, and are there separate waiting and exam rooms for sick and well animals?

Because Berners can develop allergies to contact irritants or food and their thick fur can mask inflammations or hot spots, the vet should do a comprehensive skin exam.

Ask the Expert

PROACTIVE HEALTH CARE

Q: What are proactive health steps an owner can take for her Bernese Mountain Dog?

A: "I would say two proactive things are important for Berner health. Annual physical exams and keeping their Berners fit and in good weight are the best things a family can do for their dogs."

—Debra M. Eldredge, DVM

What to Ask

Ask the veterinary staff questions. Find out about recommended vaccination protocols, the clinic's operating hours, after-hours emergency care, and the fee structure. Ask if staff members are active in their respective professional organizations and if they take continuing education courses or have certifications in canine nutrition and alternative therapies.

The Annual Vet Visit

The annual vet visit is vital for the health and well-being of your Bernese Mountain Dog. A complete wellness exam gives the vet a baseline assessment of your Berner's health, as well as any underlying or hidden health issues that can be treated before major problems develop. Done properly, a wellness visit will help your dog think of the veterinary clinic as a pleasant experience. It will also assist with a young puppy's socialization. He'll also be less likely to stress during an emergency visit if early exams are not frightening.

At the annual visit, a veterinarian will perform a physical to listen to your Berner's heart and lungs, get a baseline weight, determine joint mobility issues, and check the stool for parasites. Your dog's teeth and gums will be examined for dental disease. The vet might have specific nutrition recommendations, especially important in a rapidly growing large-breed dog like the Berner.

Because Berners can develop allergies to contact irritants or food and their thick fur can mask inflammations or hot spots, the vet should do a comprehensive skin exam. A skin examination can reveal evidence of external parasites like ticks and fleas. If you live in an area that is at high risk for these parasites, your vet will suggest a year-round preventive.

She should also look for unusual skin growths like warts or swellings that precurse cancer.

Vaccinations

As a puppy is weaned from his dam, he begins to lose certain inborn antibodies that she has provided through her milk. These maternal antibodies protect the puppy from some bacteria and viruses. A vaccination boosts the puppy's immunity at the time his natural immunity wanes. Vaccinations protect the dog from a variety of illness, such as bacterial, viral, and tick-borne diseases.

All dogs need certain vaccinations, some mandated by local or state health laws and others their veterinarian will recommend. Depending on your dog's activities, travel to other locations for dog shows, plans to board him, and requirements of training schools or groomers, your Berner might need more vaccinations than other dogs.

Prepare for a frank discussion with the vet about her vaccination protocol. Most research has proven that some vaccination protection lasts far longer than one year, the old standard. Many dogs can go three to seven years before they need boosters. Your veterinarian will suggest core vaccines, those that all puppies and dogs need, and extra protection based on your plans with your Berner.

Core Vaccines

Puppies are born with some antibodies passed from their dam, which protect the dog for a short time from some bacteria and viruses. The protection wanes during the time a puppy is weaned. Breeders usually give their puppies a first set of core vaccines. Unless a dog has a history of vaccination reaction or allergy, there is no good reason to forgo vaccination for the core diseases. These first immunizations protect against distemper and parvovirus, and the combination shot is given at six weeks of age. The first vaccine tells a puppy's immune system that a foreign body has invaded, and the immune system mounts a defense. Booster shots are given every 2 to 4 weeks until the puppy is 20 weeks old. The boosters increase the dog's immune response, and he is protected in the event of future exposure to a pathogen. The rabies vaccination is the third core inoculation for dogs, required by state and local health departments. This shot is given to dogs at three months of age, usually given separately from the combination distemper/parvovirus vaccinations.

Distemper

Distemper is a highly contagious virus that affects dogs and wildlife. Direct contact with an infected animal, or by droplets, infects a dog. Shelters and some foster homes where dogs are housed close to each other are known locations where distemper spreads.

Distemper manifests with runny eyes and nose, fever, cough, vomiting, lethargy, diarrhea, seizures, and sometimes paralysis. Puppies lose nutrients and fluids and become dehydrated. This disease can kill a very young puppy or dog who has a weakened immune system. There is no medication that will kill the virus in a dog already infected, but treatment can mitigate the dehydration, vomiting, and diarrhea. The dog must be quarantined from other pets in the home.

The distemper vaccine is effective at preventing the disease, but some puppies will still contract it. While your dog goes through the booster shot series, don't take him to training classes, pet stores, the groomer, or a dog park until his series is complete.

Parvovirus

Parvovirus, a serious and highly contagious viral disease, attacks a dog's gastrointestinal system. Parvo can cause fever, vomiting, and bloody diarrhea. The virus is spread by direct dog-to-dog contact or between a dog and contaminated stool found in yards or other environments frequented by an infected dog. This virus lives on food and water bowls, collars, leashes, kennel floors, and on the hands and clothes of people who have handled diseased dogs. Parvovirus survives for long periods in the environment because it resists heat, cold, and humidity.

A dog with parvovirus becomes dehydrated quickly, and most deaths occur two or three days after symptoms appear. A fecal test can confirm what a veterinarian suspects, but treatment can start before an official diagnosis. Fluid and electrolyte replacement, along with medications to prevent vomiting and diarrhea, are successful if begun early in the course of the disease. Some dogs develop secondary infections and are not strong enough to survive.

One of the ways in which parvo spreads is through direct dog-to-dog contact.

Any dog ill with parvovirus should be quarantined. Infection control measures for the house include disinfecting and cleaning all surfaces. Yards where an infected dog has played or pottied regularly can continue to infect a dog with parvo for several months, so dogs or puppies new to the household should be banned from any parvo-suspected areas.

Rabies
Rabies is a deadly but preventable disease spread from the saliva of an infected animal, either from a bite or scratch. As the virus spreads along the nervous system of a dog, it reaches the brain. Symptoms include behavioral changes, excessive drooling, difficulty swallowing, staggered gait, and finally seizures and death. There is no treatment for a dog who develops rabies.

Bernese Mountain Dogs who live on working farms or participate in tracking are more likely to come into contact with a rabid animal. Vaccinations provide immunity for three years at least, but some localities still require a yearly shot. Check with your veterinarian to find out what your local laws require.

Noncore Vaccines
Optional vaccinations for a Bernese Mountain Dog depend on his activities. Your veterinarian might recommend preventive shots for bordetella, canine influenza, coronaviruses, leptospirosis, Lyme disease, and parainfluenza.

Bordetella
Most boarding kennels, groomers, and training clubs require client dogs to show proof of immunization from bordetella, commonly called "kennel cough." This is a contagious disease spread by direct contact with infected dogs or from aerosol droplets. Dogs develop a dry, hacking cough, along with lethargy, fever, loss of appetite, and pneumonia. An intranasal vaccine or injection is given twice, about three weeks apart. The vaccine might be a combination inoculation for bordetella and parainfluenza, which is another bronchial illness.

Canine Influenza
Another canine respiratory virus, commonly called "dog flu," canine influenza is a contagious viral illness that spreads quickly through grooming shops, boarding kennels, training schools, pet stores, and veterinary clinics. Dog flu is contracted through direct contact with an infected dog, contact with contaminated items, or contact with people who carry the virus on their clothes or hands. Symptoms in a sick dog include a fever, runny nose, and sneezing. Canine influenza can be very serious in puppies who develop secondary infections, pneumonia, or bleeding in the lungs.

Supportive treatment like a good diet and rest may be all that is necessary. Very ill dogs might need antibiotics and supplemental oxygen.

Coronaviruses

Coronaviruses are so called because of their shape, as the virus appears to have a halo surrounding it. Diarrhea is a common symptom of the gastrointestinal type of coronavirus, while another causes a canine respiratory disease. Dogs can be exposed to these illnesses at dog shows or in boarding kennels. Most puppy mill or pet shop dogs have contracted a coronavirus and will have antibodies present in their blood. These diseases are spread by direct dog-to-dog contact and from dogs who cough or sneeze. The viruses can live on the clothes and hands of people who have handled infected dogs or on leashes, collars, and kennel surfaces.

The respiratory coronavirus symptoms are mild and include a runny nose, cough, and sneezing. Dogs can spread the disease even if they don't have symptoms. Treatment is supportive and includes adequate rest, nutrition, and hydration. Infected dogs should be isolated.

Bordetella is a contagious disease spread by direct contact with infected dogs or from aerosol droplets—it's also called "kennel cough" because it's often spread in kennels.

Canine gastrointestinal coronavirus is a leading cause of diarrhea in puppies. This virus is spread by contact with the feces of infected dogs. Puppies usually have mild illness unless they have co-infection with parvovirus. If the symptoms are severe, treatment is supportive and might include intravenous fluids. An ill dog should be isolated from other canines in the household. Commercial cleaning agents are effective to kill the virus. The dog's bedding and living areas should be thoroughly cleaned.

Leptospirosis

Leptospirosis is a bacterial disease shed through the urine of infected wild animals. If your Bernese Mountain Dog goes tracking, herding, hiking, or lives on a working farm, he can be exposed to leptospirosis through a cut or scratch in his skin, through mucous membranes in his eyes, nose, or mouth, or by drinking or swimming in contaminated water. Because rats and mice also transmit the disease, keep rodent populations under control. The leptospirosis vaccine is recommended for any dog who will be in the field or in water frequented by wild animals. The vaccine, given in two shots about three weeks apart, does not confer absolute immunity, however.

The symptoms vary; some dogs display none at all, and others are very sick with fever, vomiting, abdominal pain, diarrhea, loss of appetite, severe muscle pain, and

NEUTERING

Unless you plan to breed your Berner, he should be neutered (or spayed, if female). These surgeries can be safely done on young puppies. However, large-breed dogs like Berners can develop orthopedic abnormalities if spay/neuter surgeries are done prior to the dog reaching physical maturity. For females, this might be around the time of the first heat cycle. Dogs reach their maturity at between 9 and 15 months of age. Talk with your vet and breeder to determine the best age to neuter your Berner.

Dogs who are neutered are less likely to exhibit marking behavior, will not develop testicular cancer, and could become calmer. Female Berners who are spayed won't develop pyometra, a painful infection of the uterus. They will also cease their semi-annual heat cycle, won't attract strange dogs to the yard, and will have reduced incidence of mammary cancers.

weakness. If the disease is caught early enough, recovery is rapid.

Leptospirosis is a zoonotic disease, which means that a dog can transmit the bacteria to his owner. High-risk activities, like cleaning up an infected dog's stool, urine, or blood, carry risks of cross-contamination. Those with weakened or impaired immune systems should not take care of a dog with leptospirosis.

Lyme Disease

The Lyme disease vaccine is given to puppies at 12 weeks old, with a booster 2 to 4 weeks later. This tick-borne disease might not manifest in a dog for two to five months after a tick bite. Common symptoms are fever, lameness, joint and lymph node swelling, fever, lethargy, and loss of appetite. The illness can cause progressive kidney disease and failure, cardiac disease, or nervous system involvement. Very sick dogs can die from Lyme disease.

Treatment for Lyme disease is a long course of antibiotics, and some dogs will relapse after the first round of drugs. Some dogs develop severe arthritis and will need long-term pain relief.

Parainfluenza

The parainfluenza virus causes mild respiratory symptoms, but a dog can develop a secondary bacterial illness. Symptoms such as a runny nose can last ten days, but immunity is conferred within three or four days from the date of the vaccination. Treatment includes rest, fluids, and supportive care. If the symptoms become severe or if a secondary bacterial infection develops, antibiotics and cough control medications can be given.

Parasites

Both internal and external parasites can infect dogs at any life stage. An alert Bernese Mountain Dog owner will notice that her dog is not quite right, even if he doesn't have obvious outward symptoms.

External Parasites

External parasites can also cause illness in Bernese Mountain Dogs. Fleas, mites, ringworm, and ticks are preventable but can be difficult to treat. Weekly grooming will help detect external parasites.

Fleas

Fleas are the most common—and irritating—parasites that can infest even the cleanest dogs and their homes. These seed-sized black specks on legs live in tall and short grass, along country roads, and on urban streets. Depending on the climate, fleas can be a year-round problem or might be an occasional nuisance.

When a flea jumps on a dog, it can get comfortable, lay eggs, and feed within 24 hours. The egg larvae fall off the dog and infest the home, the dog's bedding, and the soil around the house. Larvae can cocoon for weeks before emerging as adults, and reinfestation is common.

A dog with fleas is noticeably uncomfortable. The Berner's thick black coat may hide fleas, but he can develop hot spots where he has scratched his skin. If a dog ingests a flea, he can become infected with tapeworms.

Both the dog and his environment must be treated. The house and the dog's bedding should be vacuumed daily. Linens and sofa covers should be washed in hot water. Pet-safe insecticides are sometimes used in grassy areas of the yard.

If you live in an area prone to fleas, medications or herbals prevent them from hopping onto the dog, or they cause adult fleas to die if they bite the dog.

Check your dog for fleas and ticks after he's been playing outside.

Mites

Mites are microscopic external parasites that cause illness in dogs. Ear mites, sarcoptic mange mites, and demodectic mange mites can cause ear irritation or hair loss and scaly skin patches. Disease can be mild or severe, depending on the parasite and the dog's overall health. Some are highly contagious and easily transmitted from dog to dog, making treatment very important in any dog diagnosed with mites.

Ringworm

Ringworm is an external parasite that can infect both pets and people, but it's not really a worm. Rather, ringworm is a fungal infection that gets its name from its appearance as a raised, red circle on the skin. This fungus is highly contagious and causes itching and scratching. A topical antifungal applied directly on the lesion will treat ringworm; good hygiene among family members will prevent the spread of ringworm.

Ticks

Like fleas, ticks are also found in most areas, and dogs who hike or roam in fields or on farms can be at increased risk. These

PUPPIES AND PARASITES

Puppies from even the cleanest environments can contract internal parasites from their dam during whelping or lactation. The stress of moving to a forever home can cause healthy puppies to become ill from parasites like coccidia, a microscopic germ that most dogs have in their guts. Frequent loose stools are symptoms of internal parasites. Any puppy who is lethargic, has diarrhea, or fails to thrive should be checked for parasites. Most are easily treated.

parasites live in woods, shrubs, brush, and undergrowth.

Any time a Bernese Mountain Dog has been in tick-prone areas, he should be given a thorough, hands-on tick inspection. Look around his neck, in his ears, and between his toes. To remove ticks that are already attached, grasp the tick close to the dog's skin and pull gently, making sure that the head has come out along with the body. Watch for any signs of infection where the tick was attached. Lyme disease is the most common tick-borne infection. Consider preventive medications if your Berner is active in areas where ticks are known to be prevalent.

Internal Parasites

Most internal parasites are worms that live in the dog's intestines or bloodstream. These include heartworms, hookworms, roundworms, tapeworms, and whipworms.

Heartworms

Heartworms, which are found in all US states and some foreign countries, are spread through the bite of an infected mosquito. This preventable illness can be fatal if not treated promptly. Dogs, cats, and wild animals can carry heartworm parasites, which are transmitted from an infected animal to a well animal through the mosquito vector.

When the pest bites an infected animal, heartworm microfilariae enter the insect and grow into larvae. The mosquito transmits the larvae when it bites the next victim. The heartworms mature in the dog's bloodstream, where these adult heartworms continue to mate, with the result that an infected dog will have adult heartworms and larvae that can develop and grow. The dog will cough, lose his appetite and energy, or have breathing difficulty, although other dogs show no outward symptoms. Diagnosis by blood tests and chest X-rays can confirm the presence of heartworms.

Treatment is difficult and complicated. Injections of an arsenic-based medication kill the adult worms and microfilariae. As the worms die, though, they can break off into large clumps and impair the dog's heart and lung function. A dog who undergoes heartworm treatment will need to be kept very quiet and crated as much as possible for several weeks.

Heartworm preventive won't eliminate the worms if begun after a dog has contracted the parasite, which is why your Berner's vet should test him for heartworms before starting the preventive.

Most heartworm preventives also include medication to protect a dog from hookworm, roundworm, and whipworm infection.

Hookworms

Hookworms are common parasites that bite into the dog's intestinal lining and suck blood. Hookworm larvae penetrate a dog's mouth or skin, or they are passed from an infected dam to her puppies. This parasite causes blood loss, weakness, and malnutrition. Puppies and senior Berners are particularly susceptible to severe disease. Humans in the home can also be infected with hookworms. Detection is from an inspection of the infected dog's stool. Treatment is effective with medication given for two to three weeks.

Roundworms

Roundworms are common intestinal canine parasites. Dogs become infected by eating soil that contains roundworm eggs, or by licking contaminated paws and fur, or by drinking infested water. A bitch can pass roundworm larvae to her puppies during birth or lactation.

The parasite causes malnutrition and diarrhea or pneumonia in a very young dog. A serious infestation is visible in a dog's stool, resembling long strings of spaghetti. Your dog's vet can diagnose

Roundworms are quite common in puppies.

FIRST-AID KIT

Dog owners should keep a canine-specific first-aid kit in the car and the home. Bernese Mountain Dogs who compete in sports, who work stock, or who are just too curious can suffer injuries, bee stings, or ingest poison. Essential kit items are: antibiotic ointment, antihistamine, antiseptic cleanser, bandages, blanket or large towel, blunt scissors for wound treatment, eyedropper or syringe, eye flush, gauze, hot and cold packs, hydrogen peroxide, muzzle to prevent an anxious/injured dog from biting, styptic powder, tape, tweezers, vaccination records, and your vet's emergency contact information, including poison control phone numbers.

roundworms and provide the proper de-wormer that will eliminate the infestation.

Tapeworms

Because tapeworms are usually transmitted by fleas, if your Berner has evidence of flea infestation, your vet should check his stool for tapeworms which are thin, flat, and look like grains of rice or segments of tape in the dog's stool or in the fur around his anus or tail. A dog who scoots his bottom along a rug or in the yard might have tapeworms, which can cause anemia and malnourishment. Unless the underlying flea problem is treated at the same time, a dog can become reinfected. De-wormers are very effective when treating tapeworms; your vet can prescribe the proper medication.

Whipworms

Whipworms look like tiny whips, noticeable only under a microscope. They suck blood from a dog's intestines and can cause anemia and diarrhea. Severe illness develops in young puppies or dogs who are immune compromised. Because whipworms must be diagnosed by your dog's vet, she can recommend the right medication to treat the illness. Medications also might be administered to treat the diarrhea and anemia if the infection is severe. Very ill puppies may even need a blood transfusion for severe anemia.

Berner Health Conditions

Bernese Mountain Dogs suffer from some of the same conditions seen in other large-breed dogs. Thankfully, the Bernese Mountain Dog Club of America (BMDCA) supports a program called Berner-Garde, which is an open database of Bernese Mountain Dogs who either suffer from disease or are cleared by DNA tests, radiographs, or other methods. All

Berner owners are encouraged to utilize the database to search for good breeding stock or conscientious breeders. The website and database, www.bernergarde.org, includes extensive information about health issues, research, and clinical trials. You can also find information on Berner health issues at the American Kennel Club (AKC) Canine Health Foundation's website, www.akcchf.org.

Bloat

Deep-chested large dogs, including the Bernese Mountain Dog, are prone to bloat. Researchers don't know exactly why this condition develops, but some are looking at genetic markers and environmental triggers. This veterinary emergency sometimes occurs after a dog eats or drinks, followed by hard, long exercise. The stomach dilates with gas, and the dog can develop circulatory collapse or shock. His stomach twists trapping the gas which causes excruciating pain.

A dog who develops bloat will be restless, drool excessively, try to vomit without success, and have a distended, painful abdomen. He can die if not treated in the first 30 minutes, making your actions critical. Immediately take your dog to a vet if he displays these symptoms. If his gums are pale and he weakens, wrap him in a warm blanket. Emergency surgery is vital to save a dog if he bloats.

Up to ten percent of dogs who suffer one episode will have a repeat occurrence. During surgery to relieve bloat, the vet can tack the stomach to the abdominal wall to help prevent a future episode. Also, some veterinarians recommend feeding a dog several small meals during the day rather than one large meal. If your Berner is a gulper, monitor his mealtime so that he slows down. To prevent bloat, never exercise your dog immediately after he eats.

Deep-chested large dogs, including the Bernese Mountain Dog, are prone to bloat, a condition in which the stomach dilates with gas, twisting on itself.

Cancer

Cancer kills Bernese Mountain Dogs

in huge numbers at young ages. The average age at diagnosis is six years but varies depending on the type of cancer. Recent research suggests that up to 60 percent of all early Berner deaths result from cancer. Most cancers that affect Berners are heritable and caused by many genes, which makes them polygenic. Some researchers believe that all cancers begin as inflammation on the cellular level. Environmental toxins, diet, and a dog's genetic background, might all contribute to canine cancer.

The most common cancer in Bernese Mountain Dogs is malignant histiocytosis (MH). Almost 25 percent of all diagnosed cancer cases in Bernese Mountain Dogs are MH. This nasty, aggressive disease—uniformly fatal—might manifest as a skin swelling, but it metastasizes rapidly to the liver, spleen, lungs, and kidneys.

Some of the symptoms of MH are weight loss, lethargy, weakness, and loss of appetite. A dog with MH can have trouble breathing. X-rays detect tumors in the lungs, as well as an enlarged spleen or liver. Sometimes a dog will present with enlarged lymph nodes.

There are no effective treatments for MH, and a dog diagnosed with this cancer will be given supportive treatment. Canine cancer researchers have made significant progress in some clinical trials, however. A combination of chemotherapy and immune support has increased the survival time for Berners with MH.

Elbow Dysplasia (ED)

Elbow dysplasia (ED) is a polygenic joint disease common in large-breed dogs. A dog with ED will develop painful arthritis in an affected elbow. He might limp or refuse to bear weight on the limb. Medications can control pain and inflammation. Surgical intervention is very successful to help a Berner with ED. Dogs with this condition should not be exercised hard or long and should maintain a normal weight.

Eye Conditions

Bernese Mountain Dogs are affected by the eye conditions entropion and ectropion.

Entropion causes a dog's eyelid to fit too tightly and roll inward. The dog's lashes constantly rub his cornea, which becomes inflamed and infected. Long term, a dog can become blind without surgical intervention.

Ectropion causes the eyelid to be too loose. The lower lid sags and rolls out and won't protect his eye from irritants. Chronic inflammation or infection can result. Surgery corrects the condition.

Hip Dysplasia (HD)

This heritable orthopedic disease occurs when the ball of the femur does not sit

Weight control is important for dogs with hip dysplasia because an overweight Berner is more likely to develop painful arthritis.

properly in the hip. The condition leads to pain, lameness, and arthritis. Like elbow dysplasia, hip dysplasia is thought to result from a combination of genetic mutations, making it a polygenic disease. Dogs with hip dysplasia might favor one leg, sit sloppily, exhibit stiffness when rising from a *sit* or a *down*, or be reluctant to climb stairs or walk for long distances.

Dogs can be screened for HD, either through the PennHIP evaluation or radiographs (X-rays) submitted to the Orthopedic Foundation for Animals (OFA). The PennHIP evaluation performed on puppies includes radiographs and a test of joint laxity. The Berner's age, rate of growth, and degree of laxity are figured into a formula that predicts future disease. The OFA radiographs are definitive at the time of the test but don't guarantee that the dog will not develop HD later in life. Radiographs are recommended when the Berner is two years old, where the dog's hips are rated as excellent, good, fair, or poor.

Breeders should have all of their Bernese Mountain Dogs evaluated for HD. Because this disorder can skip a generation, a wise puppy buyer will check the evaluations on her puppy's grandparents and siblings.

Surgery, exercise, and medications can help an affected dog have a good quality of life. Weight control is critical because an overweight Berner is more likely to develop painful arthritis, even if he has only mild HD.

For more information on HD, visit the PennHIP website, www.pennhip.org, or the OFA website, www.offa.org.

Kidney Disease

Bernese Mountain Dogs have an increased risk of developing a kidney disease called glomerulonephritis. This disease damages the kidneys to the point that protein is lost and kidney failure results. Dietary and medication intervention can slow the progression, but because this disease usually isn't discovered until the later stage, many dogs cannot be treated.

Von Willebrand's Disease

A form of this bleeding disorder, known to occur in Bernese Mountain Dogs, is inherited by puppies directly from their parents. Prolonged or excessive bleeding is seen during minor or routine surgery or with injuries. The disease can be diagnosed by a special blood test, which should be done when a Berner is young. If he has inherited the disorder, his owner and vet can take precautions if he suffers an injury or needs surgery. Dogs who are carriers of the disorder should not be bred to other carriers.

Alternative Therapies

Alternative therapies have gained popularity in recent years. Good science exists to support the use of nontraditional health and wellness modalities. Acupuncture, chiropractic, herbal therapy, homeopathic medicine, and physical strength and rehabilitation specialties all benefit a Bernese Mountain Dog. These therapies can help prevent illness or disease or complement traditional veterinary care.

Acupuncture

Acupuncture, the practice of placing needles in predetermined locations on a dog's body, is very effective for pain control in older, infirm, or injured Berners. The needles raise endorphin levels in the dog, which lead to relief from pain or inflammation.

Chiropractic

Chiropractic care can prevent, diagnose, or treat mechanical disorders in a dog. Berners active in agility or obedience, or who injure themselves herding or drafting, can get good pain relief after a chiropractic adjustment. The dog might be sore for another day following the procedure but will soon be back to his Berner leans and hugs.

Herbal Therapy

Herbal therapists use plants as supplements to help heal a canine or to prevent disease. Herbs can help a Berner fight infections, improve his hormonal balance, ease pain, and support healthy organs. Together with traditional pharmacology, herbal therapy can enhance a canine's well-being. Herbal practitioners work alongside your Berner's vet. Keep in mind that some medications and herb combinations are dangerous, so always ask your vet before undertaking herbal therapy for your Berner.

Homeopathy

Homeopathic therapy treats symptoms or illness with a substance that in larger amounts also causes the same illness or symptom. Prescribing homeopathic remedies should only be undertaken by a veterinary homeopath, as the remedies are complicated.

Physical and Rehabilitation Specialties

Physical and rehabilitation specialists can help hardworking Berners, obese dogs, injured dogs, or those who participate in canine sports and need to stay in top condition. Therapies include swimming, treadmills, massage, and muscle-specific exercises. A canine physical therapist can analyze a dog's gait for abnormalities in movement. Some also have subspecialties in canine nutrition. Any dog who suffers from orthopedic disease or obesity should be evaluated by a rehab or physical therapist.

Senior Dogs

Just as a Bernese Mountain Dog settles into his "good dog" years, past the age of puppyhood destruction and adolescent energy, he becomes a senior dog. The breed, tragically, is short lived, with an average life span of around eight years. A Berner earns senior citizen status as young as six years. Many Berners, however, are active well past the age of 10; some have lived beyond 14 years. Just as he has been well loved through those early years, a Berner deserves his owner's devotion during the senior years.

Illnesses

Senior dogs, like humans, are afflicted by geriatric illnesses. He might develop typical senior afflictions, like cataracts.

He may become more anxious when left at home by himself. His joints could be creaking and causing pain. He may lose his hearing. Arthritis, endocrine disorders, and autoimmune diseases can manifest in the senior years as well. Canine cognitive dysfunction (CCD), a type of canine dementia with symptoms that are similar to Alzheimer's disease in humans, is typical in dogs over the age of ten.

Because the senior Berner can't speak his owner's language, his owner must

Just as he has been well loved through those early years, a Berner deserves his owner's devotion during the senior years.

Check It Out

HEALTH CHECKLIST

✓ Take your Berner pup for well-puppy checks and vaccinations.
✓ Core vaccines protect against rabies, distemper, and parvovirus; active and traveling Berners need additional vaccines.
✓ Protect your Berner from internal and external parasites.
✓ Enroll your dog in the Berner-Garde health database.
✓ Be on the lookout for common illnesses in the Berner, such as bloat, cancer, ectropion and entropion, hip and elbow dysplasia, and von Willebrand's disease.
✓ Consider treating illness and injuries with a mix of traditional and complementary medicine.

learn to watch for subtle changes. If the dog is more vocal than normal or more quiet than usual, he could be in pain. Aggression or apprehension in an older dog can also indicate pain. Several effective therapies can help your Berner if he suffers from painful arthritis, hip or elbow dysplasia, or canine cancer.

Feeding

If your senior Berner begins to refuse food or eats much more slowly, have his teeth and gums checked for dental disease. He just might need a more palatable food or something softer than his usual kibble.

Grooming

Weekly grooming sessions take on added importance as an early detection program for certain cancers. Any unusual wart or skin growth, bumps or lumps along the dog's skeleton, or swelling that you have not felt before should be checked immediately by your veterinarian.

Activities

Enrich the senior Berner's life with low-impact activities, like a slow walk or with toys that challenge his brain. If he needs to go potty more often, teach him to ring a bell hung on the door handle. Dogs who develop deafness can be taught hand signals and given balls or other toys that light up. Conversely, if a dog begins to lose his vision, there are canine toys that beep so that he can continue to enjoy play.

Above all, put your hands on your Berner more often, lean into him, and let him know every day how special he is and how loved.

Resources

Associations and Organizations

Breed Clubs

American Kennel Club (AKC)
5580 Centerview Drive
Raleigh, NC 27606
Telephone: (919) 233-9767
Fax: (919) 233-3627
E-Mail: info@akc.org
www.akc.org

Bernese Mountain Dog Club of Great Britain
www.bernese.co.uk

The Bernese Mountain Dog Club of America (BMDCA)
www.bmdca.org

Canadian Kennel Club (CKC)
89 Skyway Avenue, Suite 100
Etobicoke, Ontario M9W 6R4
Telephone: (416) 675-5511
Fax: (416) 675-6506
E-Mail: information@ckc.ca
www.ckc.ca

Federation Cynologique Internationale (FCI)
Secretariat General de la FCI
Place Albert 1er, 13
B – 6530 Thuin
Belqique
www.fci.be

The Kennel Club
1 Clarges Street
London
W1J 8AB
Telephone: 0870 606 6750
Fax: 0207 518 1058
www.the-kennel-club.org.uk

United Kennel Club (UKC)
100 E. Kilgore Road
Kalamazoo, MI 49002-5584
Telephone: (269) 343-9020
Fax: (269) 343-7037
E-Mail: pbickell@ukcdogs.com
www.ukcdogs.com

Rescue Organizations and Animal Welfare Groups

American Humane Association (AHA)
63 Inverness Drive East
Englewood, CO 80112
Telephone: (303) 792-9900
Fax: 792-5333
www.americanhumane.org

American Society for the Prevention of Cruelty to Animals (ASPCA)
424 E. 92nd Street
New York, NY 10128-6804
Telephone: (212) 876-7700
www.aspca.org

Royal Society for the Prevention of Cruelty to Animals (RSPCA)
RSPCA Enquiries Service
Wilberforce Way, Southwater,
Horsham, West Sussex RH13 9RS
United Kingdom
Telephone: 0870 3335 999
Fax: 0870 7530 284
www.rspca.org.uk

Sports

International Agility Link (IAL)
Global Administrator: Steve Drinkwater
E-Mail: yunde@powerup.au
www.agilityclick.com/~ial

The World Canine Freestyle Organization, Inc.
P.O. Box 350122
Brooklyn, NY 11235
Telephone: (718) 332-8336
Fax: (718) 646-2686
E-Mail: WCFODOGS@aol.com
www.worldcaninefreestyle.org

Therapy

Delta Society
875 124th Ave, NE, Suite 101
Bellevue, WA 98005
Telephone: (425) 679-5500
Fax: (425) 679-5539
E-Mail: info@DeltaSociety.org
www.deltasociety.org

Therapy Dogs International (TDI)
88 Bartley Road
Flanders, NJ 07836
Telephone: (973) 252-9800
Fax: (973) 252-7171
E-Mail: tdi@gti.net
www.tdi-dog.org

Training

Association of Pet Dog Trainers (APDT)
150 Executive Center Drive Box 35
Greenville, SC 29615
Telephone: (800) PET-DOGS
Fax: (864) 331-0767
E-Mail: information@apdt.com
www.apdt.com

International Association of Animal Behavior Consultants (IAABC)
565 Callery Road
Cranberry Township, PA 16066
E-Mail: info@iaabc.org
www.iaabc.org

National Association of Dog Obedience Instructors (NADOI)
PMB 369
729 Grapevine Hwy.
Hurst, TX 76054-2085
www.nadoi.org

Veterinary and Health Resources

Academy of Veterinary Homeopathy (AVH)
P.O. Box 9280
Wilmington, DE 19809
Telephone: (866) 652-1590
Fax: (866) 652-1590
www.theavh.org

American Academy of Veterinary Acupuncture (AAVA)
P.O. Box 1058
Glastonbury, CT 06033
Telephone: (860) 632-9911
Fax: (860) 659-8772
www.aava.org

American Animal Hospital Association (AAHA)
12575 W. Bayaud Ave.
Lakewood, CO 80228
Telephone: (303) 986-2800
Fax: (303) 986-1700
E-Mail: info@aahanet.org
www.aahanet.org/index.cfm

American College of Veterinary Internal Medicine (ACVIM)
1997 Wadsworth Blvd., Suite A
Lakewood, CO 80214-5293
Telephone: (800) 245-9081
Fax: (303) 231-0880
Email: ACVIM@ACVIM.org
www.acvim.org

American College of Veterinary Ophthalmologists (ACVO)
P.O. Box 1311
Meridian, ID 83860
Telephone: (208) 466-7624
Fax: (208) 466-7693
E-Mail: office09@acvo.com
www.acvo.com

American Holistic Veterinary Medical Association (AHVMA)
2218 Old Emmorton Road
Bel Air, MD 21015
Telephone: (410) 569-0795
Fax: (410) 569-2346
E-Mail: office@ahvma.org
www.ahvma.org

American Veterinary Medical Association (AVMA)
1931 North Meacham Road, Suite 100
Schaumburg, IL 60173-4360
Telephone: (847) 925-8070
Fax: (847) 925-1329
E-Mail: avmainfo@avma.org
www.avma.org

ASPCA Animal Poison Control Center
Telephone: (888) 426-4435
www.aspca.org

British Veterinary Association (BVA)
7 Mansfield Street
London
W1G 9NQ
Telephone: 0207 636 6541
Fax: 0207 908 6349
E-Mail: bvahq@bva.co.uk
www.bva.co.uk

Canine Eye Registration Foundation (CERF)
VMDB/CERF
1717 Philo Rd
P O Box 3007
Urbana, IL 61803-3007
Telephone: (217) 693-4800
Fax: (217) 693-4801
E-Mail: CERF@vmbd.org
www.vmdb.org

Orthopedic Foundation for Animals (OFA)
2300 NE Nifong Blvd
Columbus, Missouri 65201-3856
Telephone: (573) 442-0418
Fax: (573) 875-5073
Email: ofa@offa.org
www.offa.org

Publications

Books

Anderson, Teoti. *The Super Simple Guide to Housetraining*. Neptune City: TFH Publications, 2004.

Anne, Jonna, with Mary Straus. *The Healthy Dog Cookbook: 50 Nutritious and Delicious Recipes Your Dog Will Love*. UK: Ivy Press Limited, 2008.

Dainty, Suellen. *50 Games to Play With Your Dog*. UK: Ivy Press Limited, 2007.

Morgan, Diane. *Good Dogkeeping*. Neptune City: TFH Publications, 2005.

Smith, Allison. *101 Fun Things to Do With Your Dog*. UK: Octopus Publishing Group Ltd, 2011.

Magazines

AKC Family Dog
American Kennel Club
260 Madison Avenue
New York, NY 10016
Telephone: (800) 490-5675
E-Mail: familydog@akc.org
www.akc.org/pubs/familydog

AKC Gazette
American Kennel Club
260 Madison Avenue
New York, NY 10016
Telephone: (800) 533-7323
E-Mail: gazette@akc.org
www.akc.org/pubs/gazette

Dog & Kennel
Pet Publishing, Inc.
7-L Dundas Circle
Greensboro, NC 27407
Telephone: (336) 292-4272
Fax: (336) 292-4272
E-Mail: info@petpublishing.com
www.dogandkennel.com

Dogs Monthly
Ascot House
High Street, Ascot,
Berkshire SL5 7JG
United Kingdom
Telephone: 0870 730 8433
Fax: 0870 730 8431
E-Mail: admin@rtc-associates.freeserve.co.uk
www.corsini.co.uk/dogsmonthly

Websites

Nylabone
www.nylabone.com

TFH Publications, Inc.
www.tfh.com

Index

Note: Boldfaced numbers indicate illustrations.

Photo Credits

Dedication

With love, to Leigh Anne and Mark

Acknowledgments

While researching and writing this book, I received extraordinary help from Bernese Mountain Dog owners, breeders, trainers, handlers, and judges around the country.

I especially appreciate the kindnesses extended from Sloane and W.L. Shepard, the Southeast rescue coordinators for the Bernese Mountain Dog Club of America (BMDCA). They open their home and their hearts to Berners for retraining, treatment of injuries or illnesses, and rehabilitation. Their selfless introductions to their Berner friends were a huge help to me. Their lovely rescued Berner, Rita, who honored me with a Berner lean and hug, has left us much too soon; Rita is remembered in these pages and in all the hearts of the people she touched during her too-short life.

About the Author

Linda Rehkopf is a journalist and author specializing in canine training, health, and welfare topics. She writes for several local and national animal-specific media, and her work has been nominated for the Maxwell Award for Excellence in Canine Writing. She competes with her dogs in obedience, rally, and conformation and participates in a metro-Atlanta therapy dog organization. She is a member of the Greater Atlanta Labrador Retriever Club, the Peach State Obedience and Agility Club, and Happy Tails Pet Therapy. Linda and her husband, Chris, live with their dogs in Marietta, Georgia.

NATURAL with added VITAMINS
Nutri Dent ®MD
Promotes Optimal Dental Health!

360° Design

Cleaning Action!

Dog's Love'em! ™

AVAILABLE IN MULTIPLE SIZES AND FLAVORS.

Nylabone®
Trusted For Over 40 Years

MADE IN THE USA

Our Mission with Nutri Dent® is to promote optimal dental health for dogs through a trusted, natural, delicious chew that provides effective cleaning action...GUARANTEED to make your dog go wild with anticipation and happiness!!!

Nylabone Products • P.O. Box 427, Neptune, NJ 07754-0427 • 1-800-631-2188 • Fax: 732-988-5466
www.nylabone.com • info@nylabone.com • For more information contact your sales representative or contact us at sales@tfh.com   TS446